A Practition

Upgrading to

CW01080310

5

MICH TALEBZADEH

ISBN 978-0-9563693-0-7

Table of contents

UPGRADING A GIVEN DATABASE TO ASE 15   23

THE ALL IMPORTANT ASE 15 OPTIMIZER   54

Disclaimer

Great care has been taken to make sure that the technical information presented in this paper is accurate, but any and all responsibility for any loss, damage or destruction of data or any other property which may arise from relying on it is explicitly disclaimed. The publisher and the author will in no case be liable for any monetary damages arising from such loss, damage or destruction.

About the Author

Mich Talebzadeh is an award winning Database expert with extensive DBA and Architecture experience with special interests in Sybase® and Oracle®. Mich started working on databases when he was a post graduate and has worked on Sybase since 1990s.

Mich specializes in creating database architectures for large global trading systems involving heterogeneous databases and distributed systems. He spends a good deal of his time working with Sybase and, more specifically, helping people who are using Sybase both as a DBA and developer.

Mich holds a PhD in Particle Physics from Imperial College of Science and Technology, University of London and C.E.R.N., Geneva, Switzerland. He is the co-author of "Sybase Transact SQL Programming Guidelines and Best Practices" and the author of the forthcoming books "Oracle and Sybase, Concepts and Contrasts", "The Concise Transact SQL Guidelines for ASE 15" and numerous articles.

In 2008 Mich was awarded Sybase Gold Medal for his outstanding contribution to ASE 15 [1]

Acknowledgments

I am grateful to many people for their help in completing this work. As a minimum token of my appreciation:

1. Thanks to the clients' project sponsors, infra-structure managers, project managers, developers, DBAs, data architects and UNIX specialists who took part in upgrading systems to ASE 15. We experienced a lot and achieved a lot. I am especially grateful to Robin Dighton, Jason Moles, Justin Mills, Kulvinder Mall, Geoff Hurrell, Angus Laycock, Raashid Lane, Martyn Vine, Marc Reynolds and Suda Rao for their contribution.
2. Thanks to members of ASE 15 Special Interest Forum for all the lively discussions that benefited all. I also thank the members of this forum for all their help and advice for the structure and content of this booklet.
3. I particularly like to thank Jeff Tallman, Xun Cheng, Mark A Parsons, Bill Grant, Ryan Putnam, Ed Barlow, Jack Doran, Mark Hughes, Eliezer Perl and Tom Kim for their advice and contribution to this work.
4. My thanks to Dr Raj Nathan and Irfan Khan of Sybase Inc for their continuous support over many years.

I wish you a happy reading.

Mich Talebzadeh

mich@peridale.co.uk

London, England

October 2009

ASE™ 15 ARCHITECTURE

Mich Talebzadeh
Mich@peridale.co.uk
Version 3, Jan 2006

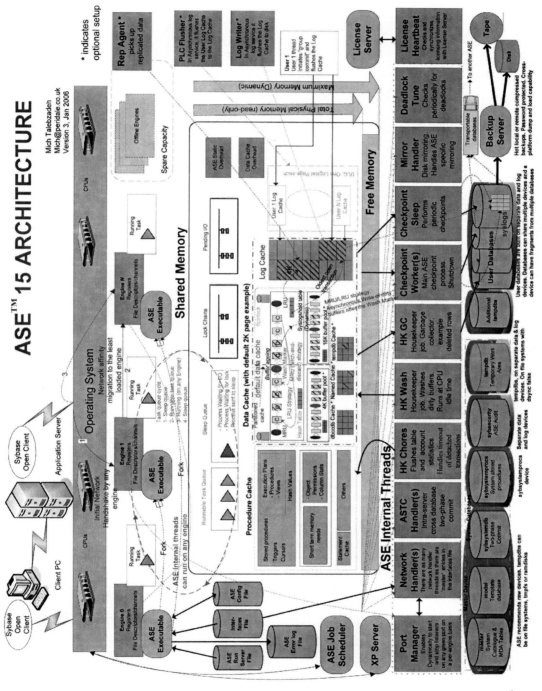

* indicates optional setup

Introduction

I decided to write this booklet after going through upgrading two major trading systems to Sybase Adaptive Server Enterprise (ASE) 15. One of these systems was Equities [1] and the other one was a Fixed Income application. I thought that there was a need to write such a booklet that focused on the practical aspects of upgrading to ASE 15, as opposed to the widely available literature published by Sybase Inc.

This is thus an aid. It is not meant to replace what Sybase officially provides nor your familiarity with your own application. However, what it provides is in line with the tried and tested steps on how to upgrade typically complex trading systems.

The target audience of this book is the Sybase upgrade team. This is the team that has hundred percent responsibilities for the successful upgrade and future performance of ASE 15. This team includes the upgrade project manager, infra-structure manager, the developers, testers, UNIX administrators and the DBA staff. This is contrary to the popular belief that the DBA is responsible for every aspect of ASE 15 upgrade and has complete responsibility over it. Since I am a fan of motor racing and Ferrari, I will use the analogy of a Formula 1 race. The DBA is the mechanic/pit-stop guy who makes sure that the fuel tank is full, the tires are replaced, the visor is cleaned and Ferrari functions as expected and ready for the remaining laps. Of course the DBA role is very crucial. A pit stop is never as easy as it looks. For seven to eight seconds (if all goes well), the drivers' chances in the race are in the hands of his pit crew/DBAs. All the racer can do is sit and wait. However, there is very little the pit-stop guy can do once the car has left the pit. It is up to the development team and testers to ensure that the car (in this case ASE 15) performs as it should and does handle those bumpy corners smoothly. In short, this ASE 15 upgrade is not just the responsibility of DBA but rather a team effort.

Let us backtrack and examine what distinguishes ASE 15 from the other previous releases of ASE. Most of us work in environments with applications that often operate under Extreme Transaction Processing (XTP), mixed Online Transaction Processing (OLTP) and Decision Support System (DSS) loads. These mixed loads are usually referred to as Operational Decision Support Systems (ODSS) these days. These applications typically have to provide a very quick response. Although we are required to answer very fast, we have to perform complex SQL statements on our databases that can be dozens of Gigabytes in size. For a long time, ASE (known earlier as Sybase SQL Server) employed nested loops joins and later on it added merge joins. The general rule of thumb, going back many years was that the nested loop join is good if at least one join's input is small or at least when indexes cover the join and the join cardinality is fairly small (i.e. 1:5). On the other hand merge join is good for two large inputs with high cardinality join (>1:10), especially where the tables are already sorted in join order (i.e. clustered on join keys) or where a predicate on the inner table can reduce the table projection to a quantity easily sorted in available memory. Hash joins work best on large tables for which no other predicates other than the join keys exist or the projections have large join cardinality, but where the input tables are too large to easily sort.

Some database systems, in particular those that targeted online transaction processing applications, did not even use merge join, never mind other join methods like hash join. This is certainly true in the early days of ASE. All join operations were executed by the nested loop algorithm. The most sophisticated join algorithm sorted the outer input and built an index on the inner input on the fly - called "reformatting" or store_index in optimization parlance. As time went by, systems had to adapt to handle both OLTP and DSS. As a result, ASE 15 introduced the hash join (HJ) algorithm. Hash join was introduced in ASE to deal with the requirements of ODSS.

Starting with ASE 15, Sybase decided to rewrite the optimizer of ASE from new. It introduced novel concepts such as n-ary Nested Loop Join (NLJs involving 3 or more tables with a close query graph) and based the new Optimizer on Volcano model with the new execution engine called Lava Execution Engine.

What all these mean to us the practitioners is that ASE 15 uses more sophisticated query-processing techniques compared to the previous versions, both in terms of the set of relational operators and algorithms implementing them. As a consequence, it is fair to say that the task of the optimizer has become harder - and thus takes longer. This is important as a full query execution involves parsing, normalization, optimization and execution - and in some cases, optimization can exceed actual execution time. Generally, optimizers handle models of query execution – and there

4

is a conceptual difference between models and practice. The best model in the world can potentially leave parts of the reality uncovered. That is, for any real life optimizer, no matter how good it is, there will always be a query, a database state and a system state where the optimizer will take the wrong decision - or will simply spend too long optimizing as compared to actual execution time. There is not such a thing as the perfect optimizer. If we agree that making occasional errors is in the nature of query optimizers, then we the practitioners need to find a way to understand the behaviour of the new ASE 15 optimizer and to cope with that.

Understanding ASE 15 new optimizer behaviour is thus important in upgrade processes. However, that is not the end to itself. In the words of a good colleague of mine, upgrading ASE 15 is not just about loading the database from an earlier version, online it and we are home and dry. As we will see later there are other factors that can make your upgrade a success or failure.

The organisation of this booklet

When I tried to push for ASE 15 in a client site in late 2007, I came across various questions and justifications from the top management that were not technical by nature. I decided then to present a cost benefit analysis of deploying ASE 15. Something that I thought could go well with less technical minds that were more interested with the value add to business (in short what business gains from this upgrade). With the benefit of hindsight that was the correct approach. So this booklet is not all about bits and bytes. It involves some business considerations that you may find applicable to your environments or you can adapt them for your own use, in order, hopefully, to facilitate your migration to ASE 15.

To keep this booklet concise and focused I have decided to detail subjects that I have actually deployed myself in ASE 15 upgrade and there are definitely certain utilities that I have not used. For example I made extensive use of Monitoring Data Access (MDA) tables readings but did not deploy any Query processing (QP) metrics. I therefore do not cover QP tuning. I also do not provide the configuration parameters for MDA settings. I therefore assume that the reader is either familiar with the MDA settings or can get some information either from myself (via email) or another resource. Of course there are others that have their own home grown monitoring scripts using Perl and other stuff. So there is a choice.

Going forward I cover various upgrade methodologies as you may care to consider. I then touch on ASE configuration settings of importance to ASE 15. We then take a route on loading a database into ASE 15 and walk through the load process. We consider such aspects as upgrading from ASE 32-bit to ASE 64-bit. Post database load we look at reorg rebuild, various aspects of statistics and consider the new ASE utility datachange() function, followed by missing statistics and histogramming steps. No upgrade is complete without detailed consideration of the ASE 15 optimizer including the join methods and optimizer switches. Since Hash Joins are new to ASE 15, we look at this join method in more details. We then cover the auxiliary utilities that you need to consider with ASE 15 upgrade, such as the correct version of Perl libraries, the SDK for UNIX and Windows and Jconnect for Websphere etc. In a complex environment there are often various types of replicated data from ASE or other sources (simple or bidirectional). We will consider replicated data from ASE 12.5.n to ASE 15 and vice versa.

No upgrade is a success without testing the code in ASE 15. It is equally important to consider how to go about testing the code as well as doing it. We will then look at planning test cycles, how to capture performance matrix, zooming on problematic SQL and so forth. ASE 15 optimizer will play a major role in the upgrade process and thus familiarity and understanding it is a must for DBAs and developers. As a DBA you may end up explaining the plan output to the developers so you will need to be sufficiently familiar with the optimizer concepts.

In the course of evaluating ASE 15 semantic partitioning we found it to be useful as a substitute to the traditional archiving. Thus partitioning besides performance benefits can potentially have other usage. This is also covered.

6

Why Upgrade to ASE15

This is a question that inevitably comes up in any conversation with the management. Is ASE 15 upgrade a high risk process with little return? Do we have to upgrade just because the end of life for ASE 12.5.4 is sometime in 2009? What are the technical and business reasons to upgrade to ASE 15, given the resources and testing time needed?

Technical Considerations

Operational Advantages of deploying ASE 15

- Eliminate/ remove specific performance bottlenecks
- Make Sybase look and feel the same across the board by allowing all the applications to be upgraded to the same version of ASE, thus getting rid of the old versions across the board
- Support for latest generation operating systems
- The new ASE 15 will make DBA support work more streamlined as it will facilitate DBAs to:
  - Consolidate to one version of ASE
  - Implement new Sybase installation standards.
  - Implement uniform housekeeping scripts across different applications
  - Retire Legacy scripts
  - Utilize new and better performance monitoring tools
  - Reduce maintenance windows over the week-end
- Maintenance jobs timing will be further reduced with semantic partitioning because the process can be done using parallelism and on the individual partitions only
- End of life in 2013.
- ASE 15 allows for data warehouse type databases to be built

Pre ASE 15 limitations

- Query optimizer costing model needed improvement
- Existing versions of ASE were 'hard-wired' for OLTP
  - Nested-loop joins and merge joins only
  - Poor or inadequate handling of DSS queries
- 256 Device limit per server and 32GB max device size limitations
- Issues with catalog contention for DDL operations, especially in temporary databases
- 30 character limit on object names
- Limitations with statement cache and ad-hoc queries

Improvements in ASE 15

- ASE 15 execution engine based on the Volcano model
- More flexibility to add new access methods
- ASE 15 execution is internally Stream-oriented rather than step-by-step oriented. This makes the result set order more efficient.
- Query optimization has been improved using new techniques such as pipelined parallelism, cost-based pruning, and timeout mechanisms as part of Volcano model
- Text replication is faster
- Key Catalogs are row-locked in all databases
- Reduced catalog contention for DDL operations
- Higher throughput for applications
- Deadlocks due to system catalog contention reduced considerably
- Improved application availability
- Increased concurrency for maintenance tasks
- Contention in the temporary work database tempdb reduced significantly
- Relieve log/cache contention
- Large identifiers, removes 30 character limit on object names
- Allows for Unsigned and 64-bit integer types
- Default network packet size = 2048 Bytes. Previous versions used 512 Bytes due to legacy network protocols
- 256 Device limit per server and 32GB max device size limitations gone

8

- Devices = 2^31; maximum device size = 4Tb
- Blocking due to stored procedure renormalization largely eliminated
- Renormalization caused by temp tables created outside proc, etc
- ASE 15 handles OLTP more efficiently

New functionalities in ASE 15

- Semantic partitioning:
  - Tables can be divided into small chunks of data called "partitions" that can be individually managed. Queries run faster because the "smart" query optimizer bypasses partitions that don't contain relevant data. In addition, one can run maintenance tasks on a subset of selected partitions which speeds up overall performance.
- Computed Columns:
  - The results of calculations can be stored in columns, saving time when applications repeat the same calculation over and over.
  - Optionally, the user or application can store the formula instead of the result, creating a virtual column that will be recalculated when it is accessed. This saves the effort of re-specifying the definition, and allows other columns to be created based on actual and virtual ones.
- Function Indexes:
  - The server can build indexes on a table based on the result of a function. When repeated searches use the function, the results do not need to be computed from scratch and the index can be used to do fast lookup based on function result.

- ASE 15.0 supports three new/improved join methods all useful for many typical applications:
  - N-ary Nested loop Join (NLJ),
    - A variant of NLJ patented by Sybase
  - Merge Join (MJ)
    - Improved from ASE 12.0 implementation
  - Hash Join (HJ)
  - Queries hitting many rows
  - Queries against star/snowflake schema
  - Queries with many aggregates

- queries joining many tables
- Queries that are not-so-well written
- SQL User Defined Functions added
- The new *instead of triggers* function improves bulk loading of data
- XML enhancements

Business considerations

Cost/Benefit analysis of migrating to ASE 15

- **Costs: (**The investment needed to realize the value of upgrading to ASE 15)

  - ➢ Implementation costs
  - ➢ Ongoing costs
  - ➢ External consultancy costs if any

- **Benefits** (The value delivered to the IT and business units by this upgrade)

  - ✓ Improved functionality
  - ✓ Reduced development cycle
  - ✓ Improved performance and query response time
  - ✓ More efficient DBA support
  - ✓ Reduced maintenance times

Other Factors

- **Data growth trends**

  - ➢ Anticipated data growth of 50-100% annually in most sites
  - ➢ Higher demands on space and performance

- **Provide value add to the development teams**

  - ✓ Enable developers to take advantage of new functionalities

✓ More efficient code, less workarounds, thus reduced maintenance cost

- **Manage and control the support resources**

  ➢ Current freeze on resources at times of rising demands with the technology dollars at premium

- **Maintain high level of availability**

  ✓ Sybase is well known for its dynamic configuration, thus allowing online changes. ASE 15 takes this further making the impact of changes to the configuration of Sybase servers on users and the applications minimal.

- **Maintain high level of scalability**

  ✓ Every single application we use in Sybase requires high availability in practice
  ✓ Some systems are 24x5 or more
  ✓ ASE 15 Cluster Edition builds on Sybase's reputation for reliability by delivering a database framework that reduces costs, improves application availability and facilitates creating a flexible data infrastructure for future business growth. An ideal solution for *mission critical* applications

- **Better server consolidation**

  ✓ ASE 15 caters for both OLTP and DSS workloads. This allows applications to use the same Sybase serves on the same hardware, thus sharing computing resources among applications. Instead of maintaining multiple copies of ASE and the OS, you only need to manage a single copy.

Some Math

- **Cost Assumptions**

11

- ➤ Working days in a Month = 20
- ➤ Uniform cost per day = £840 (£105 per hour). This is based on the total cost of a resource per typical company averaged over all resource type (DBA, developer, tester etc)
- ➤ Resource cost per week = 5 * £840 = £4,200

- **Typical Implementation costs**

Project	DBA + Data Architect resource (week)	Tester or developer Resource (week)	Batch cycle run (week)	Resource total (week)	Duration (week)	Total cost (£)
Small	1	2	1	3	4	3 * 4,200 = 12,600
Medium	3	7	2	10	11	10 * 4,200 = £42,000
Large	8-12	20-30	8	28-42	20-30	28 * 4,200 = 117,600 to 42 * 4,200 = 176,400

In addition to the above cost you are advised to add 10% contingency on the top. Consideration should also be given to indirect costs such as:

- ➤ Licensing cost
- ➤ New hardware cost

- **Benefits, tangible**

  - ✓ Improved functionality
    - – 30% functionality improvement
  - ✓ Reduced development cycle
    - – 20 % reduction in development cycle
      - **= 20 days/month*12 months*£840/day*0.2 (20% reduction)**
      - **= £40,320 annual savings per developer resource**

✓ Improved performance and query response time
  - 25% reduction in incomplete queries
  - 20% reduction in lost transactions (non recoverable)
  - 5% reduction in transactions not completed due to database not being available.

Assume 10,000 transactions per month at £100 per transaction. This leads to **10,000 * 12 * 100 *0.25*0.05* 0.2 = £30,000 annual value regained**

✓ More efficient DBA support
  - 30% reduction in the annual staff growth

= 20 days/month*12 months*£840/day*0.3 (30% reduction) = £60,480 annual savings per resource

✓ Reduced maintenance times
  - Our test on our larger databases showed on average four times faster update index statistics compared to the previous versions of ASE. Even on a conservative basis one can actually schedule the whole of the maintenance window on one weekend day, thus providing 6x24 as opposed to the usual 5x24 availability. That is 20% extra business capacity/improvement in productivity. Assume 5,000 batch transactions per month at £100 per transaction. This leads to **5,000 * 12 * 0.2 = £12,000 annual value increase**

• Summary Benefits (annual)
  - Reduced development cycle = £40,320
  - Improved performance and query response time = £30,000
  - More efficient DBA support = £60,480
  - Reduced maintenance times = £12,000
  - **Total benefits = £142,800**

Summary Cost/benefit of upgrade to ASE 15

We take an example of a typical cost for a large project (28 days) with an estimated cost of £117,600 as calculated from the above table.

```
Total cost (present value)              = £129,360
Total benefits (present value)          = £142,800
Total (net present value)               = £ 13,440
Payback period (years)                  = 0.9
Total cost (risk adjusted⁺)             = £181,104
Total benefits (risk adjusted)          = £ 85,680
Payback period (years, risk adjusted)   = 2.1
```

What the payback periods indicate is that the cost of deploying ASE 15 will be recovered at 0.9 years or at worst scenario in 2.1 years taking into account the benefits vs. the capital expenditure.

 [+] Risk adjustment is worked out at 40% above the present value of Total Cost and 40% below Total Benefits

Getting Started

Preparation Work

Preparation work is not just getting servers ready. It involves, among other things, encouraging the development teams to see the value of upgrading to ASE 15.

Regardless of other facts, ASE 12.5.4 end of life (EOL) is set at 2009. What this means is that Sybase Inc will not spend time and resources after EOL on fixing the bugs. As is customary with any other vendor, Sybase will advise you to upgrade. There are opinion holders who believe that ASE 15 is not stable enough to migrate to. You will also get the same opinion from Google surfers be it data architects, development managers or others who will insist that you are stuck between hard place and rock. Well, I do not buy that theory. We have been running a major system on ASE 15.0.2 in PROD for a year and it works fine. Those who claim that ASE 15 is not stable enough (one needs to distinguish between having few bugs and real show stoppers) are not simply making enough efforts to make ASE 15 upgrade a success. Either they give up easily or do not put enough effort in learning new and being diligent. Unfortunately ASE 15 upgrade can and will turn into a war of attrition if at any sign of an issue one runs for cover. ASE 15 upgrade like any other upgrade is not a black art, however, admittedly this upgrade requires more efforts compared to the previous ones, chiefly because it offers vastly newer options.

Thus, ASE 15 migration should be planned as a project of its own. Ideally in a larger organization a project manager should be assigned to coordinate the activities among all parties involved. The chief stake holders will be the infra-structure comprising of production support, data architect, the DBAs, the UNIX SAs and the development teams who will take part in testing and optimizing the code. It is not within the scope of this paper to go into project plans but it will be useful to consider the following:

Constraints and the critical success factors

1. Allocation of adequate time and resources by the infra-structure and development teams in order for the DBA team to carry out this upgrade
2. Agreement on the timescales
3. Resolution of all the technical and access matters
4. Keeping the deliverables and goal post constant
5. Education of technical staff on new ASE optimizer controls, diagnostics and system changes

Assumptions

As this is a high profile project, the following assumptions are made:

1. The commitment of the Senior Management to see this assignment through.
2. Resources will be available from all departments at key points during the lifetime of this assignment. These include Application developers, Application support, UNIX SAs and the assigned DBAs to this unit
3. The Relevant Managers are required to make these resources available and committed to this assignment
4. This assignment will address the point whether it is possible to create a satisfactory performance model. To this effect we expect this project to take a high profile.

I will not spend a lot on the hardware and where you should do your upgrade. If you have a spare QA server, that will be the best place to perform ASE in place upgrade or build ASE 15 from new. At the time of writing these notes we baselined our upgrade on ASE 15.0.2 ESD 6. Remember baselining is an important factor and you should ideally baseline your upgrade on the same version of ASE all the way through. For example, if you started on ASE 15.0.2 ESD 6 then ideally you should finish your tests with that version as well, as opposed to upgrading to ASE 15.0.3 half way through your tests, to avoid introducing new systematic factors.

Upgrade Methodologies

Whichever upgrade mechanism you choose, it will be unwise to use ASE 15 32-bit. After so many years of 64-bit computing, you may as well upgrade your ASE to 64-bit.

There are generally three methods that come to my mind for ASE 15 upgrade. These are:

In place upgrade

Take your current ASE 12.5.n, create a new directory tree for ASE 15 binaries and do upgrade of your ASE

Advantages:

- This method will require the least amount of space usage on target host.
- Your databases etc will be upgraded through *sqlupgrade* process.
- You do not need to worry about little bits and pieces hidden in *sysservers, sybsystemprocs* etc.

Disadvantages

- Can be touch and go at times.
- Best suited for DEV and QA servers with lower risks. It can cause surprises. I did one few years ago from 11.9.2 to 12.5.0.x. The upgrade process lost "*sa*" password half way through and the upgrade was left in limbo.
- Replicated databases need special attention (draining the log).
- The *model, master and sybsystemprocs* databases may have to be extended.
- The tempdb allocations on the master device may have to be increased to match the model database size (for system recovery purposes)
- Once you have upgraded you cannot fall back to ASE 12.5.n!

A new ASE 15 instance on the same host or a new host

You create a new ASE server on the same host or a new host (if you are migrating hardware as well). If you have enough disk space on the current host, you can create a small footprint ASE 15 on the target host and create and load devices and databases. As a caution, you should ensure that the new dataserver is created with the same page size as the existing system. ASE 15.0.3 changed the default page size to 4K to match the default OS file system block sizes as well as common SAN IO transfer frame sizes; consequently, for upgrades from existing 2K page size servers, you will need to change the default pagesize when building the new server.

Advantages

- This option provides you with the opportunity to create a clean ASE without inheriting the silly historical stuff.
- It will also enable you to create parallel replication feeds from external sources to this ASE 15 as well.
- Can also do phased migration of some databases that from an application point of view can operate independently on ASE 15.
- You can use replication server's multi-site availability (MSA) feature to entirely replicate current PROD databases to the new ASE 15 PROD. If you have confidence in your replication and do run parallel reports to prove the integrity of data, you may not need to dump and load databases as a big bang at all.
- You can also MSA your database back from ASE 15 to ASE 12.5.4 in case mid week following migration you decided to fail back to your old server.

Disadvantages

- Production support may not agree with you running parallel ASE in PROD.
- You may not have enough disk space, CPU and memory even for a small footprint database.
- Your ASE 15 will have to have a different name from PROD (although you can deploy certain tricks in here) for replication to work.

18

Upgrade using transportable databases

Transportable databases were introduced in ASE 12.5.n and allow you to upgrade one or more databases by detaching and attaching the devices containing the database or databases from your ASE 12.5.n to ASE 15. ASE 15 could be built anywhere. This technique should not be confused with the OS disk copy commands such as *dd* or snapshot technologies. The major difference is that you can use transportable database techniques without the need to shutdown ASE.

Advantages

- Pretty straight forward. Will save you disk space and dump and load hassle.
- You as a DBA can use quiesce database < tag_name > hold < dbname list > [for external dump] [to <manifest_file> [with override]] to create a manifest file and then use MOUNT DATABASE to mount these databases in ASE 15 and upgrade them.
- Handy for very large databases where dump and load over a limited upgrade weekend period is going to be very time consuming. For example for a database of 600GB, the creation of manifest file, un-mount, mount and on-line the database in ASE 15 was timed at an hour. This is in comparison to six hours that would normally take to dump and load the same database into ASE 15. That is considerable saving in time

Disadvantages

- The transportable databases are tied to the number of devices used. For example if you have a 32GB data device and a 3GB log device that contain two databases, you have to transport both databases at once. That is whatever databases are on these devices, they will be moved or their snapshot taken. In other words you pretty much have to align your databases and devices so that a device is not shared by more than one database - or that space is 'lost' when you mount the device at the other side.
- The number of databases for a set of devices migrated at one time cannot exceed eight!

- Once the devices are mounted and databases on it are upgraded, there is no going back!

 I have noticed some changes certainly in ASE 15.0.2 ESD #6 that were not present in previous version of ASE 15.0.2. For example if I try to use transportable database for a database called TRANSPORTABLE in the following example, I get the following:

```
1> MOUNT DATABASE ALL FROM '/var/tmp/manifest_file' USING
2>
'/export/home/sybase/SYB_QA/devices/SYB_QA_transportable_data.dev
'
= 'transportable_data',
3>
'/export/home/sybase/SYB_QA/devices/SYB_QA_transportable_log.dev'
= 'transportable_log'
4> go
Started estimating recovery log boundaries for database
'TRANSPORTABLE'.
Database 'TRANSPORTABLE', checkpoint=(3472262, 6),
first=(3472262, 6),
last=(3472265, 11).
Completed estimating recovery log boundaries for database
'TRANSPORTABLE'.
Database 'TRANSPORTABLE' is in QUIESCE DATABASE state. It will
recovered as for LOAD DATABASE and left off line.
Started ANALYSIS pass for database 'TRANSPORTABLE'.
Completed ANALYSIS pass for database 'TRANSPORTABLE'.
Started REDO pass for database 'TRANSPORTABLE'. The total number
of log
records to process is 46.
....
Roll forward transaction '$systshk_flush'.
Redo pass of recovery has processed 6 committed and 0 aborted
transactions.
Completed REDO pass for database 'TRANSPORTABLE'.
MOUNT DATABASE: Completed recovery of mounted database
'TRANSPORTABLE'.
MOUNT DATABASE: A new database id was required for database
'TRANSPORTABLE' in order to mount it. DBCC CHECKALLOC must be run
on this database to make corrections.
```

Note that MOUNT DATABASE: "A new database id ..." statement that now expects DBCC CHECKALLOC to be run against the database. This was not present in the previous ESDs of 15.0.2! Certainly it was not there in ESD #3 if I recall correctly.

After running DBCC CHECKALLOC you get a message

```
Alloc page 3583744 (# of extent=32 used pages=1 ref pages=0)
Total (# of extent=448000 used pages=474941 ref pages=461542) in
this database 14000 allocation pages have been corrected to match
database ID 24.
```

For a very large database (VLDB), DBCC CHECKALLOC may take a good while. I have tried DBCC CHECKALLOC after MOUNT DATABASE and before ONLINING the database and also after ONLINEING the database. It does not seem to make any odds. However, my view would be to perform DBCC immediately after MOUNTING the database and before DBCC DBREPAIR and ONLINE DATABASE commands.

Deploying transportable databases for in-place ASE 15 upgrade

There is another mechanism by which one can deploy transportable databases for upgrade of very large databases (VLDB) to ASE 15 where there are a number of constraints:

1. Consolidation of servers. No other host available for a new ASE 15
2. The timing constraint for backup and load
3. The need for upgrading individual VLDB databases to ASE 15 under control mechanism (one at a time), as opposed to in-place upgrade (through traditional upgrade methods)
4. Technical constraint. The fact that under Veritas the same disk group cannot be presented again to another ASE on the same host

My view as always is to mitigate the risk and shorten the upgrade process. Consider the situation where there are added complications like data feeds (replication) from other ASEs to this ASE. So we have a situation like this:

1. Want to start ASAP

21

2. My VLDB have their own devices (no two VLDBs share the same device fragments). That will certainly make life easier
3. Forgo the last backup process (if I can)
4. Upgrade my bare ASE 12.5 first to ASE 15 (system databases) and then upgrade individual user databases one by one through mount

Use snapshot technologies to create binary copies of your data disks. Shadow image technology is good thing to have if you use something like Hitachi® arrays. This is a feature of Hitachi arrays that makes a binary copy of a disk. There are SAN tools that allow the same. These will take a while but will allow you to create snapshot of PROD disks and present them later to another ASE 12.5 for normal backups.

Going back to PROD once the snapshot is completed, you need to un-mount that VLDB and repeat the same for all user databases until you end up with skeleton ASE 12.5 that consists of system databases and tempdbs only. Then you can perform in-place ASE 15 upgrade with little or no risk. Once this process is completed, you have an ASE 15 skeleton server. You then mount your VLDBs one by one from manifest files presenting the same Veritas® disk groups to ASE 15 this time. The mount process will assign a new database ID and will ask you to run DBCC CHECKALLOC on the database. This may take a good while. You can then bring database online that will kick off ASE 15 upgrade of that VLDB. My view would be to run DBCC CHECKALLOC before DBCC DBREPAIR and ONLINE DATABASE.

There are things that I like about this method. For example, you still have the same ASE 12.5 upgraded with all stuff saved in system tables (sysservers, syslogins etc) over years. Replication feeds into ASE will all work as usual. No DNS change etc. It is also more cost effective compared to other techniques. You even save time by importing binary statistics for the same databases done on a QA server couple of days ago. In short this gives a fair bit of time for application testers to further check the integrity of applications.

22

Upgrading a given database to ASE 15

A glance at certain ASE configuration parameters

We assume that we have a test server that is running on ASE 15. We will walk through the important configuration parameters in ASE 15 first.

max memory:

You better off to have this parameter set to 25-30% above ASE 12.5

Procedure cache size:

Remember this is important. All the extra histograms such as new statistics etc have to be loaded to procedure cache for compilation plus in-memory sorting and memory needed for statement cache (see below). Make this large. I recommend procedure cache to be around 10% of max memory. Try at least twice of what you have in ASE 12.5. Also look out for 701 error messages (out of procedure cache) in case.

default network packet size:

ASE default packet size is now 2048 bytes (used to be 512 bytes in ASE 12.5). I recommend changing the default packet size to 4096 and the *max network packet size* to 8192.

Note that like a lot of the configuration parameters in ASE 15, the default packet size is not a limit, but rather a default that can be overridden. In this case, legacy applications built using OpenClient 12.5 or previous will still connect at 512 bytes unless they are configured to use larger packet sizes.

Jeff Tallman [12] takes another view on the packet size settings. Jeff states that 2K packet size is closer to the Ethernet Maximum Transmission Unit (MTU) (1520 bytes, [13]) and in benchmarks typically performs the best. 4K packets may work best in Fibre Distributed Data Interface (FDDI [14]) or other protocols that use a larger MTU. 16K or large packet sizes work best on localhost where the IP layer MTU is not a factor - so in that case the max network packet size of 16K will be optimum.

Enable sort-merge join and JTC:

This is a depreciated configuration parameter. Merge Join is part of optimization criteria (will be covered later). JTC is always enabled and cannot be turned off in general (except for compatibility mode, introduced in 1503 ESD1).

Optimization timeout limit:

This parameter controls time spent in search engine in approx per cent of estimated execution time. 1 – 1,000 are valid values with a default of 10%. Leave it as default unless you have certain performance issues. If you want to change this do it at query or session level. Note that stored procedures optimization timeout is controlled via the configuration parameter 'sproc optimize timeout limit' - which is also a percentage with a default of 40%.

Number of sort buffers and max buffers per lava operator:

The new parameter *max buffers per lava operator* is analogous to the ASE 12.5 *number of sort buffers* parameter. However, it is applicable to both hash operators and sort operators used in Lava query plans. As a result, 'number of sort buffers' now only applies to create index and update statistics commands while query based sort operations (order by, merge joins, sort distinct), hash operators (hash join, hash distinct) and other query processing memory requirements are controlled by this parameter. The default is 2048, while a good recommended value is ten times that or 20480. Once the number of buffers has reached the max, query processing "spills" to disk in tempdb, consequently increasing this

24

value may reduce tempdb usage and query execution times. The configuration unit is server pages.

Enable matrices capture:

This parameter allows you to capture query execution metrics at server level for stuff that you could do via *set statistics [io, time] on* etc at the session level. For each database this is captured in sysqueryplans table and can be queried through sysquerymetrics view. If you want to use this feature, my advice is to turn it on at the session level. Otherwise you may end up creating so much metrics traffic that this utility itself becomes a performance bottleneck. One way to reduce the traffic is to set the filter for the capturing so that you do not end up capturing every query. As I mentioned I have limited experience of using this utility, however the advice is not to turn on this configuration parameter in production. For more information see [10].

Statement cache and enable literal autoparam:

Statement cache was introduced in ASE 12.5.2 to reduce compilation costs of queries. The statement cache stores query plans for queries to avoid a new parse of an identical query. The statement cache size is taken from the procedure cache and is a shared resource among all users.

ASE 15.0.2 literal autoparam (parameterization) adds enhancements to the statement cache. Each literal value in a query is replaced by variables. This functionality offers a better efficiency for sharing query plans in the statement cache as well as extending statement caching to insert/values statements. You will find it especially useful for replicated data or other pure OLTP queries and is strongly encouraged for ASE 15 systems for OLTP applications.

You can enable *statement cache size* by setting it > 0 and turning on *enable literal autoparam*. You can start by setting statement cache size to 100MB. Remember this is a value taken from *procedure cache* and that each cached statement is a light weight procedure and therefore an open object. Considering that the average cached statement is 1-2K, you will also need to increase the 'number of open objects' configuration

parameter by the same amount as the statement cache size. For
example, if setting the statement cache to 100MB (51,200 for the
configuration value), the number of open objects will also need to be
increased by 51200.

Imagine you have the following replicated data delivered to replicate
database

```
delete from dbo.t_raw_lh_stat_map_archive where
effective_date='20080123 00:00:00:000' and id_index=38 and
cusip='032479AC'
delete from dbo.t_raw_lh_stat_map_archive where
effective_date='20080123 00:00:00:000' and id_index=38 and
cusip='035229AL'
```

With literal autoparam the literal values effective_date='20080123
00:00:00:000' will be replaced by effective_date='@@@V0_DATE
and cusip='032479AC' with cusip=@@@V0_INT etc

You can use **dbcc prsqlcache** to print summaries of the statements
in the statement cache. For example:

```
2> dbcc purgesqlcache
3> go
DBCC execution completed. If DBCC printed error messages,
contact a user with System Administrator (SA) role.
1> select * from sysdatabases where 1= 2
2> go
1> dbcc prsqlcache
2> go

Start of SSQL Hash Table at 0x0x4c25f030

Memory configured: 10000 2k pages          Memory used: 16 2k
pages


Bucket# 376 address 0x0x4c25fbf0

SSQL_DESC 0x0x4c261040
ssql_name *ss1474809309_1275221584ss*
ssql_hashkey 0x0x4c025650        ssql_id 1474809309
ssql_suid 1            ssql_uid 1        ssql_dbid 1
ssql_spid 0
ssql_status 0x0xa0        ssql_parallel_deg 12
ssql_isolate 1            ssql_tranmode 0
ssql_keep 0            ssql_usecnt 1    ssql_pgcount 6
SQL TEXT: select * from sysdatabases where 1= 2

End of SSQL Hash Table
```

```
DBCC execution completed. If DBCC printed error messages,
contact a user with System Administrator (SA) role.
```

Number of open partitions:

In ASE 15 every table or index is assumed to have at least one partition with or without semantic partitioning. The above parameter specifies the number of partitions (in practice tables and indexes) that ASE can access at a given time via partition descriptors. This value can reach high numbers quite quickly. For example, a table with 50 partitions and 5 local indexes would use 250 partition descriptors by itself and then other tables/indexes even if unpartitioned would also each use a partition descriptor. As a result you will need to increase the default value of 500 for this setting as soon as you start using any partitioned tables - including round-robin partitioning. A good starting point is to set the value to the sum of 'number of open objects' + 'number of open indexes'. To find out the total number of open partitions you can use the following stored procedure:

```
1> sp_countmetadata "open partitions"
2> go
There are 2266 user partitions in all database(s), requiring 5201 Kbytes of
memory. The 'open partitions' configuration parameter is currently set to
5000.
```

You can use sp_monitorconfig to monitor this parameter:

```
1> sp_monitorconfig "open partitions"
2> go
Usage information at date and time: May 27 2009  9:59AM.

 Name                        Num_free    Num_active   Pct_act Max_Used
Reuse_cnt
--------------------------- ----------- ------------ ------- ----------- ----
-------
 number of open partitions        2731         2269   45.38        2305
0
```

As usual set this number to a reasonably high value like 5000 and get on with the rest.

Deferred Compilation and its impact:

It is not unusual to have cases in ASE where stored procedures and nested stored procedures create a good number of #tables or deploy local variables. Example, consider these two cases below:

1. Local variables

```
Create procedure myproc
as
    declare @v int
    select @v = avg(col5) from table t1
    select * from t2 where col1 = @v
```

2. Queries joining to #tables

```
Create procedure myproc
as
select * into #tmp from t1
select #tmp.col1, t2.col3 from #tmp, t2 where #tmp.col1 =
t2.col1
```

In ASE 12.5 the optimizer did not know about the value of local variables OR the size of these #tables. For example, ASE assumed that a #table by default had 100 rows and consisted of 10 pages. So in short ASE 12.5 optimizer made certain assumptions. This assumption although not optimal, resulted in what one could call consistent optimizer behaviour. So, regardless of the actual values of local variables or the size of #tables, the optimizer ended up with the same plan and any cached plan reuse was the same.

However, in order to deal better with these scenarios, ASE 15 now deploys a technique called *Deferred Compilation* (DC) - which is really a misnomer as what is occurring is run-time statement re-optimization. It is on by default in ASE 15 (see below for disabling options). In a nutshell with DC, the optimization of the above mentioned statements are deferred until its first execution of the statement. At that point, the optimizer will know the actual values of local variables and the size of #tables. This approach will enable ASE 15 optimizer to produce a better plan based upon the known information. When the execution ends that plan stays in cache. When the next execution happens, optimizer will use the cached plan, which may not be the best plan for the new values for local variables or #table sizes. Unfortunately this can lead to inconsistent results. So in short you will end up with scenarios that the same stored procedure produces inconsistent optimizer plans.

At the time of writing these notes, DC was under further development. The general observation is that under heavy load where deferred compilation was being done a lot, problems has been reported. Under light loads (i.e., not too much deferred compilation), it seems to work fine.

Now if you are not sure how to go about this, You may consider the following:

- Turn off deferred compilation using dbcc traceon (7730) at the query level (ASE 15.0.2+)
- Turn off deferred compilation altogether at the server level, using the configuration parameter 'procedure deferred compilation'.
- Execute the proc WITH RECOMPILE option. With this option, a DC will happen at each execution because with each execution a new plan will be generated and cached plans will not be used. This can result in a better query plan at the expense of recompiling
- Consider deploying global temporary tables whereby a permanent table is created in tempdb and all the threads access this table through views with their respective @@SPID. An example below shows this through the use of ASE 15 functions and accessing the global temporary table through a view:

```
USE tempdb
go
setuser "guest"
go
--First create the function
CREATE FUNCTION guest.mfc_sybs_sesn_id
RETURNS SMALLINT
AS
BEGIN
    RETURN @@SPID
END
go
CREATE RULE guest.mar_sybs_sesn_id
```

```
AS
    @sybs_sesn_id = guest.mfc_sybs_sesn_id()
go
--Create the underlying global temporary table
CREATE TABLE tempdb.guest.t_test_table (
    sybs_sesn_id SMALLINT NOT NULL,
    col_1 INT NOT NULL
)
LOCK DATAROWS
go
CREATE CLUSTERED INDEX t_test_table_ix1
ON tempdb.guest.t_test_table(sybs_sesn_id)
go
EXEC sp_bindrule "mar_sybs_sesn_id",
"t_test_table.sybs_sesn_id"
go
--Create view on the global temporary table
CREATE VIEW guest.v_test_table
AS
SELECT *
  FROM tempdb.guest.t_test_table
 WHERE sybs_sesn_id = guest.mfc_sybs_sesn_id()
Go
--
-- Now to test this we simply log in to ASE as
a user
-- and try it.
1> select @@SPID
2> go

 ------
     21

(1 row affected)
1> insert guest.v_test_table values (@@SPID,23)
2> go
(1 row affected)
1> select * from guest.v_test_table
2> go
 sybs_sesn_id col_1
 ------------ -----------
           21          23

(1 row affected)
1> delete from guest.v_test_table
```

```
2> go
(1 row affected)
1> select * from guest.v_test_table
2> go
 sybs_sesn_id col_1
 ------------ ----------

(0 rows affected)
--In fact the underlying temporary table where
the view --is based on can have many other
roles for other users
--
1> select * from tempdb.guest.t_test_table
2> go
 sybs_sesn_id col_1
 ------------ ----------
           16          1
           17          6

(2 rows affected)
```

ASE 15 and Disk IO hits

There have been no major changes to IO processing in ASE 15 except
the availability of big devices greater than 32 GB and support for directio
in line with what the major operating systems are offering. In general we
should negate the old views that smaller devices tend to serve our needs
better. That was due to presumption that each device is a queue inside
ASE because of file descriptor associated with the device. Therefore, by
creating smaller devices (2GB as opposed to 64GB say), you should
expect better performance. In other words largest number of smallest
disks is best for performance. Please note that my reference here is to
data and log devices and not devices for tempdb(s). In general within
ASE, once the disk IO structure is filled out for a write, it is attached to an
engine and not a device queue. As a result, more than one engine can be
submitting IO requests for the same device simultaneously (but different
ASE pages). At the OS level, I suspect it is the same as normally ASE
uses Kernel asynchronous I/O (KAIO) threads, but it may depend on the
OS, OS configuration and hardware settings. It should be pointed out that

31

an impact of fewer devices is the data cluster ratios (not meaning the calculated data page cluster ratio etc values but just in general). ASE allocates two extents by default at a time. With one device only, there will be a valid case with higher than expected fragmentation for tables.

 On a note, ASE does not stripe data across devices. It simply concatenates it. So, you will see in a lot of systems that the first tempdb fragment is never used (the 2MB allocation on master) as it quickly fills with system segment stuff. Then the first big allocation is frequently hammered until it fills, and only then does device #2 gets to play. That is why when creating a tempdb manually, it is sometimes best to create the tempdb using multiple small allocations on each device (rounding to even allocation unit sizes). So if you have a 2K system and have a 4 GB tempdb across 4x1GB devices, you will likely smack the first 1GB device to death most of the time! By allocating the 4GB in 100MB chunks round robinning the device allocations; you get better IO concurrency, assuming that is what you want (i.e. the file system devices are on different physical volumes). Of course, creating 4x1GB tempdb's (with 1 device each) and putting all into the default tempdb group so that users are round robinned between them has the same effect and the added advantage of reducing catalog contention (ASE 12.5) and log semaphore contention (ASE 12.5 & 15) [9].

In later sections we will look at a stored procedure that will take matrix on device IO hits from MDA tables

Loading a database into ASE 15

Pre-requisite

- We have an ASE 15 server. We have created a skeleton database for load with correct fragments etc.
- We assume that the database to be loaded is replicated (secondary truncation point is set)
- This database version is 12.5 something
- This database may be coming from a 32-bit ASE
- This database we call it tradingdb

The load and online sequence:

```
LOAD DATABASE tradingdb FROM 'compress::/DRIVE/SYB PROD.tradingdb.cdmp'
go

Backup Server: 4.132.1.1: Attempting to open byte stream device:
'compress::/DRIVE/SYB PROD.tradingdb.cdmp::00'
Backup Server: 6.28.1.1: Dumpfile name 'tradingdb090311286D   ' section
number 1 mounted on byte stream
'compress::/DRIVE/SYB PROD.tradingdb.cdmp::00'
Backup Server: 4.188.1.1: Database tradingdb: 455436 kilobytes (1%) LOADED.
Backup Server: 4.188.1.1: Database tradingdb: 900564 kilobytes (2%) LOADED.
Backup Server: 4.188.1.1: Database tradingdb: 1346654 kilobytes (3%)
LOADED.
Backup Server: 4.188.1.1: Database tradingdb: 1791782 kilobytes (4%)
LOADED.
....
Backup Server: 4.188.1.1: Database tradingdb: 43527454 kilobytes (100%)
LOADED.
Backup Server: 3.42.1.1: LOAD is complete (database tradingdb).
All dumped pages have been loaded. ASE is now clearing pages above page
21760000, which were not present in the database just loaded.
ASE has finished clearing database pages.
Started estimating recovery log boundaries for database 'tradingdb'.
Database 'tradingdb', checkpoint=(6895460, 25), first=(6895460, 25),
last=(6895461, 0).
Completed estimating recovery log boundaries for database 'tradingdb'.
Started ANALYSIS pass for database 'tradingdb'.
Completed ANALYSIS pass for database 'tradingdb'.
Started REDO pass for database 'tradingdb'. The total number of log records
to process is 2.
Completed REDO pass for database 'tradingdb'.
Use the ONLINE DATABASE command to bring this database online; ASE will not
bring it online automatically.
```

Note that ASE displays the load percentage as it progresses. At this stage the operation is just a straight forward load. No attempt is made to upgrade this database yet.

 ASE 15 is stricter than its predecessors. If the database is replicated you cannot *online it* without getting rid of the secondary truncation point beforehand!

Issue the command:

```
dbcc dbrepair(tradingdb,ltmignore)
go
```

```
DBCC execution completed. If DBCC printed error messages, contact a user
with System Administrator
(SA) role.
```

Now you can online the database. This is the stage that ASE 15 starts upgrading the database itself

```
online database tradingdb
go
Started estimating recovery log boundaries for database 'tradingdb'.
Database 'tradingdb', checkpoint=(6895460, 25), first=(6895460, 25),
last=(6895461, 0).
Completed estimating recovery log boundaries for database 'tradingdb'.
Started ANALYSIS pass for database 'tradingdb'.
Completed ANALYSIS pass for database 'tradingdb'.
Recovery of database 'tradingdb' will undo incomplete nested top actions.
Database 'tradingdb' appears to be at an older revision than the present
installation; ASE will assess
it, and upgrade it as required.
Database 'tradingdb': beginning upgrade step [ID    247]: verifying
sysstatistics row format
Database 'tradingdb': beginning upgrade step [ID      2]: validate basic
system type data
Database 'tradingdb': beginning upgrade step [ID      3]: alter table (table
sysindexes)
(445 rows affected)
Database 'tradingdb': beginning upgrade step [ID      4]: creating table
(table sysanchors)
Database 'tradingdb': beginning upgrade step [ID      5]: changing name of
system table (table
syspartitions, new name: sysslices)
```

This process will carry on until the upgrade is completed. The last part will display:

```
Upgrade has finished in database 'tradingdb'. ASE is now updating table
level statistics for its system
tables. Please be patient.
Database 'tradingdb' is now online.
```

Well you may ask here: is this the end of it? No, I would say this is where all the fun begins.

Tasks post completion of load and online

32-bit database matters

If the dump was from a 32-bit database, then you will need to recompile all compiled objects (defaults, rules, stored procedures, views, triggers etc) under 64-bit ASE compiler. Sybase provides a utility called *dbcc upgrade_object* for this purpose. There is a column sysprocedures.version

34

that will tell you the version of the object. For example in our case *before* upgrade the version column shows 12500

```
1> select distinct top 5 substring(o.name,1,30) AS Name, o.type, p.version
2> from sysobjects o, sysprocedures p
3> where o.id = p.id
4> and o.type = 'P'
5> order by o.name
6> go
Name                                  type version
----------------------------------    ---- -----------
P AddEvent                            P       12500
P AddSedolChkDigit                    P       12500
P ArchiveCcyFwdFormatIn               P       12500
P ArchiveCheck                        P       12500
P_AssignContractSize                  P       12500
```

Now if we run the same query following *dbcc upgrade_object*, we will notice that the version is set to 15000

```
1> select distinct top 5 substring(o.name,1,30) AS Name, o.type, p.version
2> from sysobjects o, sysprocedures p
3> where o.id = p.id
4> and o.type = 'P'
5> order by o.name
6> go
Name                                  type version
----------------------------------    ---- -----------
P AddEvent                            P       15000
P AddSedolChkDigit                    P       15000
P ArchiveCcyFwdFormatIn               P       15000
P ArchiveCheck                        P       15000
P_AssignContractSize                  P       15000
```

Generally the recompile can fail for the following reasons:

- Procedures or views addressing defunct objects like tables etc
- Procedures requiring # table existence before compilation

```
DBCC upgrade_object: Upgrading PROCEDURE dbo.abc
Msg 208, Level 16, State 1:
Server 'SYB QA', Procedure 'abc', Line 41:
#tmp not found. Specify owner.objectname or use sp help to check
whether the
object exists (sp help may produce lots of output).
DBCC upgrade object: PROCEDURE dbo.abc upgrade failed
DBCC execution completed. If DBCC printed error messages, contact a
user with
System Administrator (SA) role.
```

- Procedures requiring guest tables in tempdb, i.e. *guest.<TABLE_NAME>* and alike

Anyway you get the drift. The best bet it to get the code from the developers and recreate these failed objects again. Keep the code in a safe sub-directory and ensure that if there is a new release of a code, you will be notified and you will replace the old copy in the sub-directory.

 You are strongly advised to drop and recreate all the compiled objects once the database is loaded into ASE 15. That will ensure that all objects are compiled properly under 64-bit ASE compiler.

Reorg rebuild, dropping indexes and recreating them

Loading a database into ASE 15 should not impact fragmentation in the database objects. So as long as the dump was from a well maintained database, then I would not worry about this. You can of course run *optdiag* utility or use *derived_stat* function to measure the degree of fragmentation of tables and indexes.

 If you need to do these housekeeping operations you will be better off scheduling these tasks on ASE 12.5 server. Remember for test purposes you may decide to dump and load nightly so everything has to fit in within a schedule. If you are going live then you have a weekend to deal with all these. There may just not be enough time!

Updating statistics

As mentioned earlier on, ASE 15 databases are more reliant on up-to-date statistics than previous versions of ASE. In summary what this entails is that:

- Need to keep ASE 15 statistics up-to-date
- Use UPDATE INDEX STATISTICS as opposed to UPDATE STATISTICS
- Keep column statistics up-to-date for those columns used in joins, especially hash joins. If you cannot put index on the joining columns, you would have to use UPDATE STATISTICS on those columns or UPDATE ALL STATISTICS.
- Some documents state that you should delete statistics not used by the optimizer [7]. I will discuss this topic with other considerations further down.
- Make sure that you have enough tempdb system segment space for UPDATE INDEX STATISTICS. It is always advisable to gauge the tempdb size required in ASE 15 QA and expand the tempdb database in production accordingly. The last thing you want is to blow up tempdb over the migration weekend.
- Always use UPDATE INDEX STATISTICS WITH CONSUMERS to reduce the time it takes. This also works in ASE 12.5.4
- If you have large databases that will take longer to do UPDATE INDEX STATISTICS over a weekend, you may consider the following options:
    - You can subdivide the task by running parallel UPDATE INDEX STATISTICS on different tables in the same database at the same time. Watch tempdb segment growth though! OR
    - You can try UPDATE INDEX STATISTICS WITH SAMPLING in ASE 15 OR
    - Another favorite option of mine is to use optdiag utility as follows:

        1. Load the database into ASE 15 QA server say SYB_QA on Wednesday/Thursday before migration weekend.
        2. Run update index statistics on this upgrade database. It will take as long as it takes
        3. Use optdiag to extract statistics from ASE 15 database to a flat file
           ```
           optdiag binary statistics BigDB -Usa -SSYB_QA -o bigDB.opt
           ```
        4. Weekend of migration load the database into ASE 15 PROD server say SYB_PROD

5. Use optdiag to backup the current statistics in case you mess things up
```
optdiag binary statistics BigDB -Usa -SSYB_PROD -o bigDB.keepme
```
6. Load stats into ASE 15 PROD database from opt file you created in step 3
```
optdiag binary statistics bigDB -Usa -SSYB_PROD -i bigDB.opt
```
7. Run *sp_recompile* against the database

This should not take that long and should save you a good deal of time as well. Do not forget to use the *binary mode* of optdiag when performing optdiag. Remember the values are floats.

The use of optdiag utility assumes that the ASE 15 QA and PROD will have identical configuration parameter 'histogram tuning factor' (HTF). Prior to ASE 15.0.1 ESD#1 this value was set to 1 (by default) including that of ASE 12.5.4. The current ASE 15.0.2 ESD 6 default setting is 20 for this parameter. As long as both ASE have the same HTF value it should be fine. I suggested on the use of binary mode for optdiag. This basically means that QA and PROD servers will share the same O/S platform or at least the same Endian (Little Endian specifies that the least significant byte is stored in the lowest memory address. The Intel Pentium processor is an example of Little Endian. In contrast, Big Endian formatting takes the most significant byte and stores it in the lowest memory address. Sun SPARC processor is Big Endian).

Deleting statistics

When databases are loaded from ASE 12.5.n into ASE 15, the statistics are brought in as well. Some statistics may be out of date due to a variety of reasons. These could be columns with indexes on them in the past where the index has since been dropped. Note that dropping an index does not remove the statistics for the columns of the index from sysstatistics table. So a cleanup could be useful. Also more importantly, frequency cells introduced in ASE 12.5.2 were not used by default in ASE

12.5.n whereas they are in ASE 15.0. This is reflected in the change of the default value for 'histogram tuning factor' changing from 1 to 20. As a result, the actual number of histogram steps could be up to 20 x the number of requested steps. This potential order of magnitude increase in histogram steps not only can impact the amount of procedure cache necessary to cache the statistics, it can also greatly increase optimization time as the time it takes to find the correct histogram cells increases proportionately with the number of cells. Since update statistics inherits old requested step counts, the result often is an unintended extremely large histogram step count. Thus if you suspect this is the case and you have confirmed this as part of your testing process, deleting old histograms will remove these old step counts and will allow new histograms to be created with the new frequency cells and out-of-range statistics capability (see below) In that case, first, identify unindexed columns that have statistics. Then backup existing statistics using optdiag or by bcp'ing systabstats and systatistics. Further delete all existing statistics and run fresh update index statistics maintenance plus the statistics on unindexed columns identified in step one.

Note that normally deleting statistics should not be done while the application is online as queries that are optimized during this period will be forced to use the optimizer 'magic numbers' instead. Consequently, this step of deleting the index statistics and re-creating the stats should be done as part of the upgrade process and if it has been confirmed in your testing process as a necessary step. After updating the statistics, use a query similar to the below [10] to review the actual number of steps vs. data item cardinality to determine if too many steps exist - in all cases you should try to avoid more than 1,000 total steps.

```
-- Check for ActualSteps > 500,
-- Check for Stale Statistics (more than 14-30 days old)
select TableName=object name(ss.id),
        ColumnName=col name(ss.id,convert(int,substring(ss.colidarray,1,2))
),
        Row Count=st.rowcnt,
        RequestedSteps=convert(int,ss.c5),
        ActualSteps=convert(int,ss.c4),
        ApproxDistincts=convert(int,round(1/convert(double
precision,ss.c15),0)),
        DistinctsPerStep=round(convert(int,round(1/convert(double
precision,ss.c15),0))
                                /convert(float,convert(int,ss.c4)),0),
        Uniqueness=str(1.0/(convert(double
precision,ss.c15)*st.rowcnt),12,10),
        RangeDensity=str(round(convert(double precision,ss.c2),10),12,10),
        TotalDensity=str(round(convert(double precision,ss.c3),10),12,10),
```

```
       UpdStatsDate=convert(varchar(20),moddate,100),
       DaysAgo=datediff(dd,moddate,getdate())
from sysstatistics ss, systabstats st
where ss.id > 100 and st.id > 100
   and ss.id=st.id
   and ss.formatid=100
   and st.indid in (0,1)
   and ss.c4 is not null
order by TableName, ColumnName
```

Datachange function, what it means and what it can do

I have written extensively on datachange function in Sybase forums and have decided to incorporate all these here. When we talk about datachange we are referring to the function datachange() introduced by Sybase in ASE 15. Reference [3] discusses the theoretical foundations for datachange function. It states:

For a column i in a table O that has n rows, let I be the number of inserts, D the number of deletes and U the number of updates. The datachange for column i, $DC(i)$ is calculated as:

```
DC(i) = (I + D + 2*U)/2
```

For object O, for example a table, the datachange at object level is calculated as:

```
DC(O) = ( MAX((I + D + 2*U) for each column i having
statistics)) / n
```

Now if we look closely to what the above formula says, we notice that there is a rather simplistic assumption that all columns with statistics are important, or rather valid. That is if you have any stale (meaning out of date) data, it will be picked by this function since the value of datachange for this column will be cumulative and that will be the highest scorer on the list (as indicated by MAX in the formulae above)

With stale statistics the results will be inaccurate at least as you have to go back and find out which column was the culprit and remove the stats for that column manually. As such my view is that the datachange function at table level as defined above is not representative.

Going forward I think it *will be far more practical not to use the default DC(O),* and define our own version *with selected columns,* for example, only column 1, and column 3 are included, but not column 2, *even if it has statistics*, we could then have:

```
USER_DC(O) = MAX(datachange(<TABLE>, null, <COLUMN_1>),
datachange(<TABLE>, null, <COLUMN_3>))
```

The question is what defines selected columns in the above formula? We should simply select the following columns:

1. For a given table work out datachange function for a table DC(O) based on datachange for columns DC(i) with existing *histogram entry*
2. For datachange for columns DC(i)s make sure that you are looking at columns where histogram was updated recently (say in the past week). That is deterministic
3. Find out the MAX(DC(i) among all those columns qualified for a table
4. Set UD DC(O) = Max(DC(i) for qualified columns)

So I decided to write the following stored procedure to do what I wanted a user defined datachange function to do. The code has some notes to explain what the procedure does.

```
use sybsystemprocs
go
IF EXISTS (SELECT * FROM sysobjects WHERE  name =
"sp__UserDCTable" AND type = "P")
    DROP PROC sp__UserDCTable
go
CREATE PROC sp__UserDCTable (
                            @objname varchar(255)=NULL
                            ,@days int=NULL
                            ,@format char(1)=NULL
)
AS
--------------------------------------------------------------
------------------------------------------
-- Vers| Date  |       Who            | DA | Description
-------+-------+---------------------+----+----------------
------------------------------------------
-- 1.0 |22/02/09| Mich Talebzadeh      |    | initial version
```

41

```
-------+--------+-------------------+----+-----------------
--------------------------------
/*
The datachange function monitors DML activities and measures
the number of
INSERTS, DELETES and UPDATES on an object, column or
partition since update
statistics was last run. The function measures the changes
to data distribution as a
percent of number of rows in the table or partition.
To keep track of the changes to the data distribution, three
internal counters are
maintained, one each for INSERTS, DELETES and UPDATES. These
counters are
maintained per partition. They are stored in the partition
descriptor and cached inmemory.
The in-memory values are flushed to disk periodically
through an idlesoaker
thread. As the counters are available in-memory, no
additional I/O is required
to maintain them.
For a column "i" in a table "O" that has "n" rows, let "I"
be the number of inserts,
"D" the number of deletes and "U" the number of updates.
Then the datachange for
column "i", "DC(i)" is calculated as:
DC(i) = (I + D + 2*U)/2
For object "O", the datachange at object level is calculated
as:
DC(O) = ( Max((I + D + 2*U) for each column "i" having
statistics)) / n
Whenever there is a DML on the table, the corresponding
counter is incremented.
The counters are reset when statistics are updated for the
object/partition or during a
clean shutdown of the server.
datachange function for a table in the calculation below is
based upon the existence
of statistics for columns where a histogram exists and
modification date > preset value.
In that case the routine finds the max DC(i) and bases the
user defined DC(O) = max(DC(i))

  This procedure takes optional tablename and the what stats
to look for >@days as optional
```

42

```
  parameters. By default it will only consider those columns
that have histograms less
  than 7 days old in the calculation of DC for table

  EXEC sp__UserDCTable  -- for all table with histograms <
one week
  EXEC sp__UserDCTable t_holding_analytic,14 -- for table
t_holding_analytic with histogram < 2 weeks

-------+--------+--------------------+----+-----------------
----------------------------------
*/
BEGIN
set plan optgoal allrows_oltp
set nocount on
create table #indexes (index_name varchar(255), keylist
varchar(255))
if @days is null
  set @days = -7   -- stats less than 7 days old
else
  set @days = -@days

if @objname is not null and object_id(@objname) IS NULL
BEGIN
        print "no such table %1!",@objname
        return -1
END
create table #tmp (TableName varchar(30), ColumnName
varchar(30), HistogramDate datetime, CustomDataChange
numeric(10,0), IndexName varchar(30) null)
insert #tmp
  select substring(object_name(c.id),1,30) AS TableName
  ,substring(c.name,1,30) AS ColumnName
  ,s.moddate AS HistogramDate
  ,convert(numeric(10,0),maxx.CustomDataChange) AS
CustomDataChange
  ,null
  FROM (
  SELECT
        object_name(sc.id) AS TableName
        ,max(datachange(object_name(sc.id),null,sc.name)) AS
  CustomDataChange
  from
        sysobjects so
        ,syscolumns sc
        ,sysstatistics ss
```

```
  where so.type = 'U' and so.sysstat2 & 2048 != 2048 -- only
local user tables
  and so.id = sc.id
  and object_name(sc.id) is not null
  and ss.id = sc.id
  and convert(tinyint, substring(ss.colidarray, 2, 1)) =
sc.colid
  and ss.formatid = 102
  and ss.sequence = 1
  and ss.moddate > dateadd(day,@days,getdate())
  and object_name(sc.id) =
isnull(@objname,object_name(sc.id))
  group by object_name(sc.id)
  ) AS maxx
  inner join syscolumns c on object_name(c.id) =
maxx.TableName
  and c.id in (select id from sysobjects so where
so.type='U' and so.sysstat2 & 2048 != 2048)
  and datachange(object_name(c.id),null,c.name) =
maxx.CustomDataChange
  inner join sysstatistics s on c.id = s.id and
convert(tinyint, substring(s.colidarray, 2, 1)) = c.colid
and s.formatid = 102 and s.sequence = 1
  and object_name(c.id) = isnull(@objname,object_name(c.id))
if object_id(@objname) IS NOT NULL
BEGIN
  If upper(@format) = 'V'
  begin
    exec sp__getindex @objname
    update #tmp
    set IndexName = substring(i.index_name,1,30)
    from #tmp t, #indexes i
    where i.keylist like '%'+ColumnName+'%'
    select distinct * from #tmp -- where CustomDataChange >
0
    order by CustomDataChange,TableName,ColumnName
  end
  declare @CustomDataChange numeric(10,0)
  SELECT distinct @CustomDataChange  = CustomDataChange from
#tmp
  if @CustomDataChange is not null
    return @CustomDataChange
  else
    return 0
end
else
```

44

```
BEGIN
   --
   -- Work out index columns in #tmp table
   --
   create unique clustered index #tmp_uci on
#tmp(TableName,ColumnName)
   declare @TableName  varchar(30), @ColumnName varchar(30),
@IndexName varchar(30)
   declare index_cursor cursor
        for
        select   TableName
                ,ColumnName
                ,IndexName
        from     #tmp
        for update of
                        IndexName
        open index_cursor
        fetch index_cursor
        into
                        @TableName
                       ,@ColumnName
                       ,@IndexName

if ( @@sqlstatus != 2 )
begin

        while ( @@sqlstatus = 0 )
        begin
                delete from #indexes
                exec sp__getindex @TableName
                if @@error !=0 or @@transtate = 3
                begin
                        if @@trancount > 0 rollback tran
                        raiserror 20009 "Could not get
values"
                        return
                end
                update #tmp
                set IndexName = substring(i.index_name,1,30)
                from #tmp t, #indexes i
                where
                        t.TableName = @TableName
                and     t.ColumnName = @ColumnName
                and     i.keylist like '%'+@ColumnName+'%'
                if @@error !=0 or @@transtate = 3
                begin
```

```
                              if @@trancount > 0 rollback tran
                              raiserror 20010 "Could not update
#tmp table"
                              return
                    end
                fetch index_cursor
                         into
                          @TableName
                          ,@ColumnName
                          ,@IndexName
        end
        if (@@sqlstatus = 1)
        begin
                if @@trancount > 0 rollback tran
                raiserror 20011 "#tmp Table cursor error"
                close index_cursor
                deallocate cursor index_cursor
                return
        end
end
close index_cursor
deallocate cursor index_cursor
  select distinct * from #tmp -- where CustomDataChange > 0
  order by CustomDataChange,TableName,ColumnName
  return 0
END
END
go
```

This stored procedure sp__UsrDCTable for a given table will return the percentage volatility for the table based on the max value of datachange for a given column. That column is the one that histograms are updated (based on @days parameter). The value of datachange for a column will increase as we go along and not do update statistics. It will go back to 0% if stats for all qualifying columns are done. So if today the proc returns a value of 569 it means that (as shown below), the volatility in these columns has been 569% (since last update stats).

```
1> exec  sp__UserDCTable t_instrument_alt_code,null,v
2> go
 TableName
ColumnName                        HistogramDate
CustomDataChange
```

```
--------------------------------   --------------------------------
--  ------------------------  ----------------
  t_instrument_alt_code
alt_type_id                                   Feb 23 2009
10:16PM                569
  t_instrument_alt_code
alt_value                                     Feb 23 2009
10:16PM                569
  t_instrument_alt_code
instrument_id                                 Feb 23 2009
10:16PM                569
(return status = 569)
```

If I perform sp_helpindex on this table (as below), all these three columns are used in indexes so doing an update index stats will sort out the need. This table has 296,635 rows. The volatility is high because the % change is high based upon the smaller number of rows. That is where the decision comes. If the table is only 300,000 rows who cares! You will just do the index stats and any column stats needed

```
1> sp_helpindex t_instrument_alt_code
2> go
Object has the following indexes
  index_name                 index_keys
index_description
--------------------------   -----------------------------  -------
------------  ----------------------
  ncl_alt_value              alt_value
pk_t_instrument_alt_code   instrument_id, alt_type_id
nonclustered,
  index_01                   alt_type_id, alt_value
nonclustered
```

Now let us look at a reasonably large table (rows). The last time we did update index stats for this table of 147 Million rows was on 15th Feb.

```
1> exec sp_spaceused t_holding_analytic_hist
2> exec sp__UserDCTable t_holding_analytic_hist,14,v
3> go
  name                    rowtotal   reserved    data
index_size   unused
```

47

```
 ------------------------ --------- ----------- ----------- -
 ---------- ---------
 t_holding_analytic_hist 147706879 76539340 KB 55374748 KB
20498500 KB 666092 KB
 TableName
ColumnName                            HistogramDate
CustomDataChange
 ------------------------------- -----------------------------
-- -------------------------- ----------------
 t_holding_analytic_hist
data_src_cd                             Feb 15 2009
5:28PM                  2
 t_holding_analytic_hist
fund_index_id                           Feb 15 2009
3:11PM                  2
 t_holding_analytic_hist
instrument_id                           Feb 15 2009
4:37PM                  2
```

Again these are all indexed columns. The volatility is only 2% since Feb 15. So I will leave it as it is (knowing that ideally I should be looking at hitting 10% change (hot spot for arguments)) to do this stats update. ! That will save me a bit. It will take good few hours to perform update index statistics on this table anyway.

Other examples of stored procedure sp__UserDCTable usage are as follows:

```
1> /*
2> shows various ways the SP returns value(s) for datachange
function DC(O) for a table
3> based upon User Defined DC(O) = max(DC(i) for significant
columns for that table
4> A significant column means it has a histogram (formatid =
102) and moddate > certain date
5> */
6> declare @v int
```

```
7> exec @v = sp__UserDCTable t_event_log    --- returns DC(O)
for a table with histograms < 7 days old (default)
8> exec @v = sp__UserDCTable t_event_log,8 --- returnd DC(O)
with histograms < 8 days  old
9> exec @v = sp__UserDCTable t_event_log,8,v --  show
details of columns that satisfy DC(O), verbose mode
10> --
11> -- table level User Defined DC(O) for a given database
12> --
13> set rowcount 5
14> exec sp__UserDCTable -- show me details of DC(O) for all
tables < 7 days
15> exec sp__UserDCTable null, 14 -- show me details of
DC(O) for all tables < 2 weeks
16> go
(return status = 0)
(return status = 5)
 TableName
ColumnName                         HistogramDate
CustomDataChange
 -------------------------------- ---------------------------
-- -------------------------------- ----------------
 t_event_log
event_level                            Feb 18 2009
12:34PM                 5
 t_event_log
event_time                             Feb 18 2009
12:34PM                 5
(return status = 5)
 TableName
ColumnName                         HistogramDate
CustomDataChange
 -------------------------------- ---------------------------
```

49

```
-- ------------------------- ----------------
 t_aggregate_holding
eff_dt                                   Feb 21 2009
10:34AM                    0
 t_aggregate_holding
instrument_id                            Feb 21 2009
10:34AM                    0
 t_benchmark
benchmark_id                             Feb 21 2009
9:00AM                     0
 t_benchmark_source
benchmark_src_cd                         Feb 21 2009
9:00AM                     0
 t_benchmark_type
benchmark_type_id                        Feb 21 2009
9:00AM                     0
(return status = 0)
 TableName
ColumnName                         HistogramDate
CustomDataChange
 ------------------------- ---------------------------
-- ------------------------- ----------------
 t_aggregate_holding
eff_dt                                   Feb 21 2009
10:34AM                    0
 t_aggregate_holding
instrument_id                            Feb 21 2009
10:34AM                    0
 t_event_log
event_level                              Feb 18 2009
12:34PM                    5
 t_event_log
event_time                               Feb 18 2009
```

50

```
12:34PM                    5
 t_fmw_macro_instructions
instruction_id                          Feb 18 2009
12:34PM                   20
(return status = 0)
```

 I think volatility is the right word to use for datachange function. Also there is really not a mathematical correlation between the number of changes and quality of statistics. That is:

- datachange does not imply lack of quality statistics.
- Whereas, good statistics, then bad, do imply datachange.

I mean, in reality so what if the data changed! Ok, your column data was modified by x% based upon the summation of inserts, 2*updates, deletes and total current record count. I need to know what percent of statistics were lost, would cause a change in query plan, or have caused an inaccuracy of any histogram value within some error of say 10%.

), it is not the data changes that warrant statistics update. It is the lack of quality statistics which warrants that. The statistics/histograms by themselves are useless to an operator who does not know how to use them. It takes analysis of the statistics to determine if based upon your queries, indexes, columns used in equijoins, nature of data changes (not that just a data change happened), that helps determine whether or not statistics should be modified. Through analysis of your objects and the type of activities that could cause statistics/ histograms to become inaccurate, you can determine your course of action.

Histogram steps

We have already covered this topic earlier on under section dealing with "Deleting statistics". This is another consideration that touches statistics and data distribution in the histogram. It deals with the quality of statistics stored for a given column. A column can have low cardinality or in another words a small number of distinct values. For example gender column, being male or female. In other scale a column with high cardinality means a lot of distinct values. For example trade_ID column that identifies a trade uniquely.

ASE 15 by default uses 20 histogram steps. That is reasonable for small tables or low to medium cardinality columns. However, for large tables, this value may be too low. If you believe that increasing histogramming step will provide more accurate statistics and hence better performance, then you can delete the old statistics and create with larger steps. For example:

```
delete statistics ${TABLE NAME}
go
update index statistics ${TABLE NAME}
USING 400 VALUES
WITH CONSUMERS=10
Go
sp recompile ${TABLE NAME}
go
```

Yes I know. Some will say that UPDATE STATISTICS will perform SP_RECOMPILE implicitly. Call me old fashioned but I would rather do it explicitly anyway.

In the above example we are using 400 steps for the histogram. In general you should not increase the number of steps beyond 400. Remember there is a cost attached to this as well. It will take longer for the optimizer (at compilation time) to load a histogram for a table with 400 steps compared to loading the same with 20 steps (Histogram Tuning Factor (HTF) could give you more accurate histogram but with less number of steps in the final histogram compared to simply increasing the step count.

Missing statistics

In ASE 15 you will be able to identify missing statistics by setting the following flag

```
set option show missing_stats on
go
```

If you set this flag up, you will get a report of missing stats in the log file. For example:

```
NO STATS on column tradingdb..t_process_status.status
NO STATS on column tradingdb..t_process_status.process_type
NO STATS on column tradingdb..t_process_status.task
NO STATS on density set for tradingdb..t_process_status={status,
process_type, task}
```

Out-of-range histogram feature in ASE 15

You may have come across potential issues of rapidly growing tables with monolithically increasing date values and statistics coverage. In some cases this resulted in statistics for this column being out of date mid-week into business. I remember a case of a table of order of 500 million rows with 24 million new instrument entries a day in ASE 12.5.n. This date column happened to be the leading column of a couple of indexes in that table. The nature of the application was that it relied heavily on dynamic SQL and as such stored procedure caching was not feasible. In order to provide a work-around for performance issues, the table statistics had to be renormalized mid week for this column. The idea was to stop the optimizer using the magic numbers to estimate the statistics for this column. We basically used optdiag to extract the statistics from the table, then modifed the entries to add another histogram bin to reflect the new entries for this data column. We then used a spreadsheet or a simple program to ensure that the sum of Weight values for 21entries (i.e. 20 default bins + 1 added bin) added up to 1 or 100%. This was performed by renormalizing the entries. Once the normalization was done, we put the modified information for this column statistics back into the database using the optdiag facility. Obviously that solution was far from ideal but managed to mitigate the performance issue mid-week.

Now going back to out-of-range histogram feature in ASE 15, according to ASE documentation [16] column statistics for rapidly growing tables may become out-of-date when an update statistics command completes. This results in out-of-range SARGs (search clauses) that select a greater range of values than described by the column's histogram. ASE 15.0.2 ESD 4 added this feature to give some selectivity for those columns that are growing in an increasing fashion. It could avoid zero row underestimation and reduce the need for frequent update statistics. However, the potential drawback of this feature is that it could make some index scans more xpensive, which would discourage index scans.

The syntax is as follows:

```
update statistics table_name (column_name)using out_of_range
[on | off|
default]

on - Enables out-of-range histogram adjustment for
column_name.
off - Disables out-of-range histogram adjustment for
column_name.
default - Affects the out-of-range histogram adjustment
depending on
the value of trace flag 15355
```

Traceflag 15355 turns off this utility server wide (NOT at the session level only). There are drawbacks for turning off this utility. So, I would be hesitant about using this trace flag.

The All important ASE 15 optimizer

It is impossible to perform a successful upgrade without understanding the implication of optimizer choices and switches in ASE 15. We will look at what is generally available to optimizer in ASE 15.

I would like to explain briefly about the three join methods; namely *nested loop join*, *merge join* and *hash join*.

54

Nested Loop Join

I start with the *nested loop join* (NLJ) as it is the easiest to visualize, and the one whose cost calculation is best known.

Consider the following query

```
SELECT
          T1.col1,
          T2.col2
FROM
          Table1        T1,
          Table2        T2
WHERE
          T1.colx = <VALUE>
AND
          T2.id1 = T1.id1
```

If we tried to write a code to emulate a NLJ on these two tables, it may well look like the following:

```
for r1 in (select rows from Table1 where colx = <VALUE>
loop
   for r2 in (select rows from Table2 that match current row from
Table1)
   loop
       output values from current row of Table1 and current row of
Table2
   end loop
end loop
```

Looking at this code, you can see two loops. The outer loop works through Table1 and the inner loop works (possibly many times) through Table2. Because of the structure of this pseudo-code, the two tables in a nested loop join are commonly referred to as the outer table and the inner table.

 The term *outer* and *inner* are really only appropriate to nested loop joins. When talking about hash joins, you ought to refer to the *build* table and *probe* table. For merge joins, the terms *first table* and *second table* are sufficient

Nested loop join will be chosen if one of the tables is small and the other table has an index on the column that joins the tables.

There are three variants of nested loop join:

- Simple NLJ, a search that scans an entire table or index.

- Index NLJ, a search that performs lookups in an index to fetch rows.

- Temporary index NLJ with reformatting, a search that uses temporary index (index, which was created by query execution engine and was destroyed when the query completed).

Since nested loop joins are familiar to most readers, I would not elaborate on them anymore.

Merge Join

The logic behind the *merge join* (MJ) relies on the fact that *ordered joins* provide clustered access to joining rows. Thus this type of join (when conditions are met), results in less logical and physical I/Os. Additionally, with merge join, one can exploit indexes that *pre-order rows on joining columns*. MJ is particularly suitable for DSS type queries where both the first and second tables can be large. If the second table is sorted on the join key, then the access will be efficient. For example, in Figure 1 below, both tables T1 and T2 have clustered indexes on the join column. In this case, the query is a prime candidate for a merge join. You can think of merge join as taking two sorted lists of values and merging them.

Table T1   Where T1.pk=T2.pk   Table T2

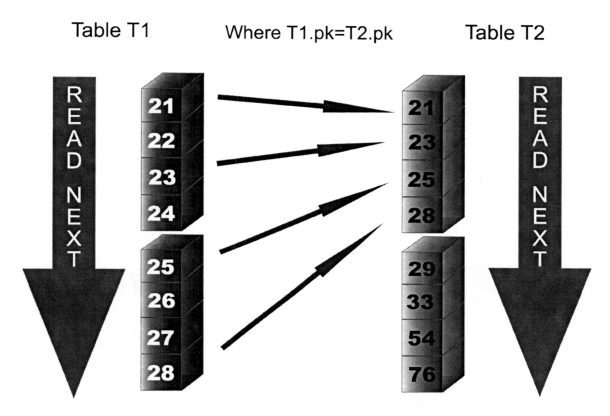

Figure 1, illustrating a merge join

The type of merge join selected depends on the join keys and the available indexes. In ASE, merge join is broken into four distinct types:

- Full Merge Join
- Left Merge Join
- Right Merge Join
- Sort Merge Join

With the parallel processing there will be eight merge join possibilities as each type mentioned above can be done in parallel as well.

Sort Merge Join

In the case of *sort merge join* where there is no useful index in either table on the join column of the two tables; ASE predictably creates a worktable for each. When a worktable is created for a merge join that requires a sort, only the columns that are needed for the result set and for later joins in the query execution are selected into the worktable. Then these worktables are sorted on the keys corresponding to joining columns and the result is merged as shown in Figure 2 below.

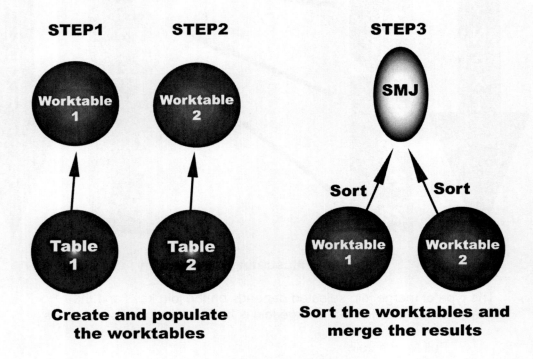

Figure 2, Steps involved in sort merge for tables with no useful index

ASE will use the available sort buffers if it can, to create the worktables in memory. This can eliminate the physical reads associated with worktables that are traditionally created on the *system segment of tempdb*.
Depending on the size of the data sets and the availability of sort buffers, spillage may happen and ASE may have to use worktables on tempdb as well. The other important aspect of merge join is that the merge join will

make its ordering available to its parent operator. This may turn up to be very cost effective in the context of the overall cost of the query.

Hash Join

From a practical point of view, a hash join comes to play when you tend to join two tables with a large set of information (large being a relative term). The smaller of two tables is hashed into memory. Unlike merge join, a hash join is equally efficient when no useful index exists on the join column in either input. We will come to that later.

In a nutshell, when we do a hash join, we acquire one data set and convert it into the equivalent of an in-memory hash table (assuming that we have sufficient resources), using an internal hashing algorithm on the join column(s) to generate the hash key. Hashing allows the execution engine to determine whether a particular data item matches an already existing value by dividing the existing data into groups based on some property. You put data with the same value from the first table in what is referred to as a *hash bucket* (see below). We then start to acquire data from the second table, applying the same hashing function to the join column(s) as we read each row, and checking to see whether we can locate a matching row in the in-memory table. Since we are using hashing function on the join column(s) to randomize the distribution of data in the hash table, one can appreciate that a hash join can only work when the join condition is equality.

From this brief intro a number of points are deductible:

- The hash join can be used even if *there are no adequate indexes on the joined columns.*
- Hash join is most efficient when one of the tables is significantly different in size to the other one. I have to be careful when I use this statement. The comments about *small and large or different only makes sense in terms of small and large data sets extracted from the tables by the query.*
- Hash join gives best performance when the build table can be hashed into memory. This is fairly unambiguous. If you manage to do your operations in memory, it will be much faster than accessing worktables on disk.

Conceptually a hashing algorithm works in the following way:

- It takes a set of inputs
- Applies a hash function F(X) to the join key known as the *hash key*. According to [4], ASE uses *modulo* or to be more precise (*mod 20*) (i.e. <JOIN_COLUMN> % 20) to work out this value. The result of using a *hash function* on a *hash key* is called a *hash value*.
- This function returns a consistent (deterministic) value. For example, F (13776) will always return a hash value of 16 during this query.
- The algorithm creates a hash table based on hash values.
- According to [5], in ASE, the *hash value* itself is not stored in the hash table. It is used as an offset into the hash table's start. The hash table construct is created in ASE's procedure cache [5]. However, it is clear that with (mod 20); the maximum number of offsets is going to be 20, i.e. in the range between 0-19.
- We have to account for hash collisions as well. The set of inputs is potentially many (definitely not known until we encounter them all). For example, F(12416) and F(13776) can both hash to offset 16.
- ASE uses the smaller input (data set), called the *build input* or *build stream,* to actually build memory structures called *hash buckets*. It is reasonable to assume that each offset of the hash table will be associated to one bucket.
- In simplest form these hash buckets are built into memory buffers (assuming we have enough of them). Otherwise the optimizer will use the worktables on the specific tempdb that is allocated to the user
- These buckets are actually stored as linked lists, in which each entry contains only the columns from the build input that are needed.
- The best optimization is achieved by having as few collisions as possible, thus saving the optimizer going through the linked list to retrieve multiple rows for the same offset value.
- Then, one row at a time, the hash join operator inspects the other input and tries to find a matching offset. The second input is called the *probe input* or *probe stream*. If a match is found, the qualified rows consisting of columns from the *build* and or *probe* inputs will

be passed to the parent/Emit operator, otherwise the row is discarded.

Hash join Dynamics, memory requirements and restrictions

You may be wondering how does the optimizer determine which table is smaller and hence should be chosen as the build table? *This goes to the point of having useful and up-to-date statistics available to the optimizer.* To effectively use hashing, ASE must be able to make a good estimate of the size of the two inputs and choose the smaller one as the build input. It would help if the optimizer knows statistics about these two tables well. This is a case in which column statistics can be helpful. Statistics can tell the optimizer the estimated number of rows that will meet a given condition, even if there is no actual index structure to be used.

 ASE has the ability [6] to switch the build and the probe input streams. Sometimes, during the execution, the execution engine will discover that the build input is actually the larger of the two. This could happen due to out of date statistics or skewed data. The execution engine can then actually switch the roles of the build and probe input midstream, in a process generally known as *role reversal.*

The hashjoin operator can use up to 128 buffers for building a hash table in memory (that is what has been claimed/reserved). The claimed buffers will actually be allocated only as they are needed. To explain the difference between *claimed* and *allocated* would require more words. In short, *claiming* only will not affect the database page caching until the reserved are actually *allocated.* The configuration parameter *maximum buffers per lava opeator* sets an upper limit for the number of buffers used by Lava operators that perform sorting or hashing. These Lava operators use buffers from the session's *tempdb* data cache pool as a work area for processing rows. The default configuration setting is 2048 buffers or 2048 x 512 bytes or 1 MB. There is a property displayed in the output of Lava Operator Tree called buffer count or bufct (displayed when you turn on *set statistics plancost on*). How is this bufct number decided? Here is the rough logic. The *claimed* number is static for the sort operations and hash joins. That is, it is determined at compile time based on the estimate of the input set size. The claimed number is dynamic for group_hashing and distinct_hashing. That is, additional buffers will be claimed on an as needed basis. In both these cases, the maximum number of buffers that can be claimed is bound by:

```
MIN("max buffers per lava operator",
("max resource granularity" *
<number of pagesize buffers in session's tempdb>) / 2)
```

ASE by default will claim a minimum of 128 buffers regardless of the estimate if there is only a single complex operator in the plan and it is a hash operator.

What happens if ASE cannot provide enough sort buffers needed for the hash join? In this case, the hash join may run out of memory during the build phase. If it runs out of memory, ASE must split the input into partitions (not to be confused with table partitioning), each containing a set of buckets, and write those partitions out to worktables on disk. The hash join keeps track of which "partitions" of the hash table are still in memory and which ones have been spilled to disk. As the operator reads each new row from the build table, it checks to see whether it hashes to an in-memory or an on-disk partition. If it hashes to an in-memory partition, it proceeds normally. If it hashes to the worktable, the operator writes the row to disk. This process of running out of memory and spilling partitions to disk may repeat multiple times until the build phase is completed.

The operator performs a similar process during the probe phase. For each new row from the probe table, it checks to see whether it hashes to an in-memory or an on-disk partition. If it hashes to an in-memory partition, the optimizer probes the hash table, produces any appropriate joined rows (projection), passes them to the parent or Emit operator as the case may be and discards the row. If it hashes to an on-disk partition, it writes the row to disk to the corresponding probe partition. Once the optimizer completes the first pass of the probe table, it returns one by one to any partitions that it spilled. Each partition (with a particular set of hash buckets) is brought into memory and read. This increases the amount of work required in terms of I/O and general processing time. It then reads the build rows back into memory, reconstructs the hash table for each partition, and then reads the corresponding probe partitions and completes the join.

The hashing and merging strategies can be much more memory intensive than the nested loops strategy, and since the query optimizer takes into account all the available resources, It will not come as a surprise that a system with little available memory might not use the hash and merge joins as often as systems with plenty of memory.

A glance at the optimizer switches

optgoal allrows_mix

This is the default out of the box mode, will consider nested-loop-joins, parallelism (needs to be enabled) and merge joins. This mode will not consider hash joins or bushy tree plans

optgoal allrows_oltp

This will consider nested loop joins and serial plans only but will not consider merge joins or hash joins etc.

optgoal allrows_dss

This will consider nested loop joins, merge joins, hash joins and bushy tree plans based on costing. This is nearest to what I call fast throughput.

optgoal fastfirstrow

This preference sets the optimization goal to retrieve the first record as quickly as possible. Table below shows the default settings for various optimization criteria.

Default settings for optimization criteria				
Optimization criteria	fastfirstrow	allrows_oltp	allrows_mixed	allrows_dss
append_union_all	1	1	1	1

Default settings for optimization criteria				
Optimization criteria	fastfirstrow	allrows_oltp	allrows_mixed	allrows_dss
bushy_search_space	0	0	0	1
distinct_sorted	1	1	1	1
distinct_sorting	1	1	1	1
group_hashing	1	1	1	1
group_sorted	1	1	1	1
hash_join	0	0	0	1
hash_union_distinct	1	1	1	1
index_intersection	0	0	0	1
merge_join	0	0	1	1
merge_union_all	1	1	1	1
multi_gt_store_ind	0	0	0	1
nl_join	1	1	1	1
opp_distinct_view	1	1	1	1
parallel_query	1	0	1	1
store_index	1	1	1	1

Warning: ASE 15.0.2 and ASE 15.0.3 versions currently do not support *fastfirstrow* optimization mode.

Auxiliary Utilities and their Compatibility with ASE 15

Besides database upgrade, there are many other items that will need reviewing. Among them are:

1. Certifying a correct version of OpenClient (SDK) on UNIX that works correctly with ASE 15
2. Certifying a correct version of OpenClient (SDK) for windows that works correctly with ASE 15 including .NET, ODBC and JDBC drivers
3. Testing Websphere connectivity
4. Sybperl and Perl DBI
5. Replication to and from ASE 12.5.n to ASE 15

We will go through this list one by one

Version of OpenClient (SDK) on UNIX

```
Sybase CTISQL Utility/15.0/P/DRV.15.0.0/SPARC/Solaris 2.8/BUILD1500-
050/OPT/Mon Jul 11 18:26:08 2005
```

Version of OpenClient (SDK) on Windows including .NET, ODBC and JDBC drivers

The following version on Windows

```
Sybase CTISQL Utility/15.0/P-EBF14167 ESD #7/PC
Intel/BUILD1500-093/OPT/Wed Dec 13 20:04:04 2006
```

Pure SDK 15 was failing against ASE 15.0.2 using .net drivers

We applied a subset of ebf (that is the drivers for .net). The EBF used was EBF 15138 for Windows x86 32-bit, part of Conn 15.0 ESD #11 release dated 05 Nov 2007 Software Developer Kit.

The dynamic link libraries (dlls) that worked were:

```
sybase.data.aseclient.dll (available in both SDK 12.5 and
SDK 15) and
sybase.adonet2.dll (comes with SDK 15 only)
```

Sybase ODBC drivers:

```
Sybase ASE ODBC Driver 4.20.00.15
```

Sybase JDBC drivers:

```
jConnect-6_0
```

Testing Websphere connectivity

Websphere uses Java. You will need jconn3.jar. A copy of which is available from ASE 15 installation subdirectory:

```
$SYBASE/shared/lib/jconn3.jar
```

Sybperl and Perl DBI

We had issues with Perl modules (Perl 5.6) running against ASE 15.0.2 using ASE 15 client on Solaris. Sybperl modules were working fine with V 5.6 and ASE 15 client but Perl DBI was failing with core dump. After discussion we were advised to compile Perl 5.8.8 with ASE 15 Open client.

The UNIX SA then downloaded and created a completely new Perl bundle 5.8.8 including rich featured modules. DBI, DBD, XML etc. The components were as follows:

```
Perl 5.8.8 version for Solaris
Sybase CTISQL Utility/15.0/P/DRV.15.0.0/SPARC/Solaris
2.8/BUILD1500-050/OPT/Mon Jul 11 18:26:08 2005
```

The developers tested all the Perl modules including **Perl DBI** and they all worked fine with 5.8.8.

Worth noting that DBD:`:Sybase binary (the Sybase.so) was originally built for Sybase Open Client 12.x so most likely why it was not working with Open Client 15.

Replication to and from ASE 12.5.n to ASE 15

ASE 12.5.4 to ASE 15.0.2 via Replication Server 12.6

This should work fine

ASE 12.5.4 to ASE 15.0.2 via Replication Server 15.01

This should work fine

ASE 15.0.2 to ASE 12.5.4 via Replication Server 15.01

This functionality is supported as long as you do not use any features of ASE 15.0.2 that is not included in your ASE 12.5.4. The list includes:

- bigint and unsigned int/smallint
- unicode text
- large table/column names > 30 char
- computed columns
- any ASE 15.0.2 specific DDL (e.g. partition by range, function indexes, etc.)
- stored procedure source code containing ASE 15.0.2 optimizer directives (e.g. set plan optgoal allrows_oltp)

The stuff that will only work for ASE 12.5.4 but not anything below:

- encrypted columns
- integer identity

 Avoid replicating DDL. For example, you can add functional indexes in ASE 15 whereas that index type does not exist in ASE 12.5.4. You might even be able to fudge with some of the datatypes if you use the repdef mapping capability - i.e. use bigint datatype in ASE 15 and map it to a numeric so that 12.5.4 still works.

Testing SQL Code in ASE 15

Now we focus our attention on how to go about testing SQL code in ASE 15. This is a job that needs to be done in close collaboration with testers and developers. However, there are occasions that you will need to do the test as login with *sa_role* yourself.

There will be many occasions where the code will behave OK. In general as a ball park figure you should expect 20-40% improvement in code running in ASE 15 compared to ASE 12.5. As a result one would expect three different scenarios, namely:

1. ASE 15 code run faster than ASE 12.5
2. ASE 15 code runs more and less the same as ASE 12.5
3. ASE 15 code runs considerably slower than ASE 12.5

I guess you will need to be more concerned with points 2 and 3. However, every test needs to be prepared and done systematically. Complex queries or procedures should be narrowed down to the section of the code that takes longest. This may involve some work for developers to get the data ready. Any statement of the code that does DML; for example, UPDATE through complex joins, should be run first as SELECT through the same joins to see if the joins are the bottlenecks etc. So let us go through this process first.

Recommended to do list

It is almost impossible to have blanket recommendations that fit every scenario. However, the following should help

- Get the code in a format that can be tested
- Turn on MDA tables and make sure that you are reasonably familiar with MDA readings and can make sense of them. Alternatively deploy other monitoring tools
- Establish that ASE is not starved off. For example, check the size of procedure cache to make sure that it is a reasonable size. Check that the named caches are created with relevant buffer pool sizes etc. In short is ASE 15 server configured appropriately?
- Check that you have run UPDATE INDEX STATISTICS on all ASE 15 databases
- Do not change the optimization mode at the first hurdle. There is no magic solution there
- Recommend the following switch and set commands for testing the code

```
select @@optgoal
go
set switch on 3604   -- the old dbcc traceon(3604)
go
--
```

```
-- Ignore forced joined orders and other forced options in the code
--
dbcc traceon(15307,15308)
go
--
-- Print out missing statistics if any
--
set option show missing stats on
--
set showplan on
set statistics time on
set statistics io on
set statistics plancost on
go
```

 There is an alternative debugging tip for use. Put the following switches in one line

```
set statistics plancost, resource, time, io on
go
--
-- your query here
--
set statistics plancost, resource, time, io off
go
```

This will display the query tree with estimates (logical, physical, rows and CPU) at each level. More convenient in reading the debugging output.

The following additional set commands that may come handy

```
--
-- turn off parallel queries
--
set parallel query off
go
--
-- turn off statement cache usage
--
set statement cache off
go
--
```

```
-- Flush the procedure cache if you want a new plan. Beware
this will
-- get rid of anything else from procedure cache otherwise
use WITH
-- RECOMPILE OPTION
--
dbcc proc_cache(free_unused)
go
--
-- You can run the procedure without actually executing it
--
set noexec on
go
--
-- You can run the query without data returned back to the
client
--
set nodata on
--
-- set tracefile for SQL running for a given process SPID
say 11
--
set tracefile '<DIR>/sql.txt' FOR 11
```

- Remember set flags will show you the matrix about the code but will not show the overhead from the system tables in parsing and compiling the code. For example, major system table overheads include loading the histograms for various user tables in the query and CPU efforts needed to create and dissipate #tables. The outcome would be that MDA tables reading will be more realistic in terms of overall cost of running the query than the optimizer readings.
- My recommendation is to wrap the query in a stored procedure and execute the stored procedure code instead, if necessary WITH RECOMPILE option. Imagine I would like to test the code in a procedure below. This is the way I will go about testing the code for a procedure called *abc* in database *tradingdb*.

```
declare @start datetime
select "==> Started on tradingdb.. abc at " +
convert(varchar(25),@start,109)
exec tradingdb.. abc @i_eff_dt='20090331' ,@i_inst_hold_flag ="I" ,
@i_data_src="MLYNC"
select "Finished on tradingdb.. abc code, Time taken in milliseconds = " +
convert(char(20),datediff(ms,@start,getdate()))
print ""
exec sp_monitor 'procedure', 'tradingdb', 'abc', 'detail'
print ""
go
```

A sample output from sp_monitor will look like this:

```
ProcName                    DBName AvgElapsedTime AvgCPUTime AvgWaitTime
AvgPhysicalReads AvgLogicalReads AvgPacketsSent NumExecs
--------------------------- ------ -------------- ---------- ----------- ------
---------- --------------- -------------- --------
 abc tradingdb          751060      13901.0           0.0              0.0
3233447.0        1026.0          1
```

The above gives the summary of the most important parameters as needed.

Optimization switches at session and query levels

You are strongly recommended not to change optimization settings at server level and instead use optimization settings at the session level. The following describe various optimization goal settings at the session level:

```
set plan optgoal allrows oltp

set plan optgoal allrows mix

set plan optgoal allrows dss
```

You can use the same switches at the query level as well. For example

```
set plan optgoal allrows mix
..
...
..
select t1.c1, t2.c5 from t1,t1
where t1.c6 = t2.c4 plan '(use optgoal allrows  oltp)'
```

The way optimization goals work are as follows:

- Query level settings override both session and server wide settings
- Session level settings override server wide settings

Optimization Criteria

72

You can also use individual optimization criteria as needed within the session level itself. Imagine you have turned on allrows_dss but you do not want the optimizer to consider merge joins. In that case you can switch off merge-joins by setting the following:

```
set merge join off
```

So the way the criterion works is by using the on/off switch. Other relevant set criteria are as follows:

```
set merge join on/off
set hash join on/off
```

Which optimization goals to use

ASE optimizer compares alternative plans in its search space to find the best plan for a given query. Depending on the search space and the settings, optimizer varies in the compilation time and the quality of the execution plan it can generate. There have been many opinions expressed on this. One [7] recommends setting the optimization goal to allrows_oltp presumably as it states for the simple reason that this optimization goal resembles ASE 12.5 behaviour. Well I will take a different view on this. If the objectives of the exercise were to simulate what ASE 12.5 did, then there is no point in upgrading! Thus, a more pragmatic approach would be to keep the default out of the box optimization goal as allrows_mix. My reasoning is that in realities most systems are a mix of OLTP and Batch. OLTP will benefit from the traditional OLTP settings and the normal batch joins will benefit from other optimizer offerings such as merge-joins.

So in summary keep the optimization goal as default (allrows_mix). The newer versions of ASE 15 (for example ASE 15.0.2 ESD 6) have a more stable optimizer and earlier problems observed have (by and large) been rectified. Bear in mind that wider optimization goals such as allrows_dss will take more time to create the query plan (compilation time) as they consider wider options. The objectives would be that although the optimizer will have a longer compilation time, one should end up with a better plan and hopefully shorter execution time.

In order for the optimizer to figure out the optimal execution plan, the followings are considered:

- The syntax of the statement
- Any conditions/predicates that the query has specified (the WHERE clauses)
- The underlying objects that the statement needs to access
- All possible indexes that can be used in retrieving data from the table(s)
- The set statements used (server-wide, session specific or query specific)
- The TSQL specific statements such as force index, degree of parallelism, prefetch size etc
- All available objects statistics generated with the UPDATE INDEX STATISTICS command
- The physical table location in case of distributed query

Running stored procedures with SP_RECOMPILE option

During testing periods, you may decide to change optimizer settings and run stored procedures. If you do not flush the procedure cache with *dbcc proc_cache(free_unused)* or similar, there is a good chance that the optimiser will use the old plan already in the procedure cache. The easiest method (as opposed to reboot of ASE, running *sp_recompile* on user tables etc) would be to execute the stored procedure with SP_RECOMPILE option to ensure that ASE creates a plan with the new optimizer settings. However, this has some limitations. *The reason is that SP_RECOMPILE only recompiles the highest level stored procedures.* If they are nesting stored procedures, for example Proc A calls Proc B and Proc B calls Proc C, neither Proc B or C will be recompiled, unless both Proc A and Proc B codes are modified to execute the Proc B and Proc C *with RECOMPILE* option as well. Be aware of this issue.

Planning test cycles

It is vital that you plan your test cycles systematically and decide collectively with your developers and production support teams on how to go about doing the test. From my experience it is essential that you pay attention to the daily and overnight batch cycle runs. The daily OLTP stuff (point queries) tends to deal with fewer records and should behave normally. However, the daily index reports or overnight batch runs can reveal various performance issues if any.

Baselining data

Assuming that you have an ASE 15 test server ready, you would ideally need to compare the results of batch runs with ASE 15 against PROD or an ASE 12.5 server with similar set up to that of ASE 15. Bear in mind that performance is a deployment issue and you are unlikely to be able to create the same conditions as PROD in a test environment. However, you should be able to apply what I call scaling factors to be able to compare your results with that of PROD or any other ASE on 12.5.

In most cases it will not be realistic to do a daily load of databases from PROD to 15 server and run the batch jobs. Remember that every load from PROD to 15 will have to go through the upgrade process that roughly involves:

- Load and online the database, removing secondary truncation point etc
- Dropping and recreating compiled objects
- Applying UPDATE INDEX STATISTICS to the database

In practice the frequency of these loads need to be adjusted to your individual needs. However, it is mostly true that a weekend load of databases, where in most probability all business activities are finished Saturday AM, would be most realistic, in terms of comparing apple with apple. For example, your 15 server databases are synched with PROD over the weekend and you run batch jobs on PROD and 15 servers Monday morning. You will then be able to compare the results and confirm that the 15 server performs the job not only in a timely manner but results also tally. This is very important in case you have modified ASE 15 code for performance reasons.

Maintaining basedlined data

Once databases are loaded to ASE 15, then you will need to maintain them the way you maintain your PROD. For example run UPDATE INDEX STATISTICS and REORG COMPACT as necessary. One of the frequent mistakes that people do is NOT pruning data from daily log tables in ASE 15 etc as they do it in PROD. This normally results in slower performance on ASE 15 databases as test cycles continue. Use MDA readings to measure daily DML activities on ASE 15 tables and compare them with those of PROD. A 24 hour cycle measurement should be good. If you notice that certain tables have different DML hits (insert/update/delete) compared to PROD you will know that either ASE 15 is not doing everything in terms of batch activity (some jobs are missing), or there is something inconsistent somewhere.

Test cycles

The objective of test cycles is to ensure that from performance measurements point of view one is focusing on CPUs and logical I/Os and eliminating physical I/Os as much as possible. In line with other performance tests, it is advisable to run a cycle at least twice or better three times one after the other, keeping the baseline the same and ensuring the cache stays warm (i.e. not rebooting ASE after each cycle). This may be easier said than done. If that is the case and you may end up rebooting ASE or flushing the cache, notes should be taken on the use of physical I/Os and these should be compared for each cycle.

Test cycles generally should address two concerns. These are:

- The performance matters
- The consistency of results

DBAs generally have a lot of input in dealing with performance issues. In contrast, the DBAs have little to do with the consistency and accuracy of the results. This is the domain of business analysts or production support.

76

If you have a batch cycle involving many jobs, my suggestion is to let the cycle complete, noting down timings for individual jobs. From our experience the slowness of certain jobs can be traced back to a certain part of the code or one or two procedures called by many parent procedures. It is also equally likely that some jobs under some data conditions will perform differently timewise. For example, a job may run fine under normal conditions but can exhibit slow response when covering a condition in the code that will force it to go through different logic, thus invoking a different procedure. If a job does not finish in a reasonable time, then you may have to simply red flag the job and kill it allowing the cycle to continue.

Once the upgrade team have compiled the list of jobs and their timing in ASE 15 (an Excel sheet will do), it is prudent to compare the timings with those from PROD or another server running ASE 12.5. At the first cut those jobs running faster or on par with that of ASE 12.5 should be filtered out and the focus should be on those running slower. In practice you will likely end up with a mixed bag with certain jobs running faster, the same and slower.

What matters is not one job but the whole cycle

In any upgrade process consideration should be on the macroscopic level as opposed to micro level. For example if the full batch cycle in PROD takes 8 hours and the same in ASE 15 takes 6 hours, with 80% of jobs running faster and 20% slower (none being show stoppers), then it is a win situation despite the 20% slower tasks. It will be unrealistic to expect every migrated code to ASE 15 to run faster. So what matters is the overall timing. If the overall timing is acceptable to the business and they sign it off then the upgrade can be carried out and the slower running code can be assessed post migration if needed.

Performance matrix capture

These are server and code level performance matrix that need to be captured on a daily basis by the DBA. These are:

- Server level Matrix

1. ASE engine utilization
2. Memory utilization
3. Cache utilization
4. Locks, blocks, long running transactions, #tables and their size, stored procedures in the cache and the compilation time etc

- Application level Matrix
  1. Average procedure statistics
  2. Table and Index usage analysis for each database
  3. Tempdb utilization per job

It is not within the scope of these notes to describe the methods and tools to obtain the above info. However, it is possible to get most of this matrix from MDA readings. An interesting one is plotting the engine utilization. An example is shown below. I particularly like this plot as it quickly reveals the spike caused by various batch jobs.

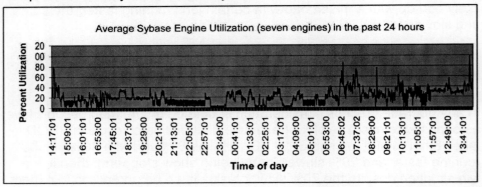

CPU intensive activities can also be caused by capturing large amount of query plan metrics at server level. Be aware of this and make sure that you do not create additional resource bottleneck.

I mentioned Average Procedure statistics. You will also need to capture matrix pertaining to procedure statistics. An example is shown below. You may also be interested in measuring the Average CPU time. Also it would be useful to measure the number of executions of a stored procedure.

Procedure	No of Executions	Average Elapsed Time/ms	Average Logical I/O	Average Physical I/O
<DB>..P_GetInstrHoldings	6	1109908	61903	10
<DB>..P_GetBondEuroBatchTNC	2	914460	5683	0
<DB>..P_ValidateIdxData	14	664325	120242867	1281
<DB>..P_CreateBBRatingReq	2	326853	9162451	7795
<DB>..P_LoadIdxStructure	8	267136	3108	0
<DB>..P_ValidateIdxProfile	6	251402	5561263	117

Going about dealing with problematic code

Dealing with slow running code in ASE 15 is really no different from dealing with any other slow running code, except that we need to remember that ASE 15 offers newer options. As a DBA, you will need to have the right game plan in place for finding and fixing problem SQL code in ASE 15. Fortunately, ASE is good at providing information in the system and MDA tables, to help a DBA locate and analyze potentially bad SQL, so by using the roadmap and scripts provided in this booklet; you should be able to identify any bad SQL that is executed in ASE 15. It therefore makes sense to define what we mean by problematic SQL (P-SQL). What criteria can we use when we begin to look for problematic coding?

Our first step is obvious. Say, during testing process we found out that a given stored procedure takes far longer to complete compared to ASE 12.5. This could be a border line procedure in ASE 12.5 that had an acceptable performance but in 15 exhibited far worse response. In latter parts we will consider examining the output from showplan and Lava Execution Engine.

Narrowing down the code

Try to narrow down the code to the section that is causing the problem. This can be identified through looking at the long running transactions and locks held on certain tables (see below). You can also quickly use *sp_showplan <SPID>,null,null,null* to see where the code is hanging. Another crude but effective way is to modify the code, put print markers at sections of the code and see where the code (make sure that you cover all the logical conditions) is failing and take it from there. There may be occasions that the problematic query depends on the results from previous sections. If that is the case, arrange with developers to prepare a temporary table with the intermediate results and join the query with temporary table.

Parameters to consider

What follows are some general criteria you can use when evaluating the output from various database monitors or home grown diagnostic scripts.

- **Overall Response (Elapsed) Time -** how much time the query took to parse, execute, and fetch the data needed to satisfy the query. It should not include the network time needed to make the round trip from the requesting client workstation to the database server.

- **CPU Time -** how much **CPU time** the query took to parse, execute, and fetch the data needed to satisfy the query. The CPU Time in this case is measured within Sybase and directly refers to throughputs of Sybase Engine(s), as discussed earlier.

- **Physical I/O -** often used as the major statistics in terms of identifying good versus problematic SQL. It is a measure of how many disk reads the query caused to satisfy the user's request. While you certainly want to control disk I/O where possible, it is important that you not focus solely on physical I/O as the single benchmark of inefficient SQL. Make no mistake, disk access is slower than memory access and also consumes CPU time making the physical to logical transition. However, you need to look at the entire I/O picture of a SQL statement, which includes looking at

80

the logical I/O as well (see below). One of the major problems in this area is the lack of proper indexing for the query resulting in a table scan or inefficient joins, for example Cartesian joins.

- **Logical I/O** - a measure of how much cache reads the query took to satisfy the SQL request. The goal of tuning I/O for a query should be to examine both logical and physical I/Os, and use appropriate mechanisms to keep both to a minimum. What can cause large logical I/Os? An example would be having a non-unique clustered index on an all-pages locked table which may result in excessive overflow pages as each key can have many rows. Thus a single insert results in multiple logical I/Os.

- **Repetition** - a measure of how often the query has been executed. A problem in this area is not as easy to spot as the others unless you know the application well. A query that takes slightly longer in ASE 15 to execute can cause a headache on your system if it is executed erroneously over and over again. An example would be a query that executes in a loop. Repetition can also cause issues by the fact that although the individual process does not take that long to complete, the process executed multiple times can consume a large amount of resources within ASE.

Looking for Clues

Long Running Transactions

More often than not the worst possible case for a P-SQL is that the process sits on a table longer than it needs to, and hence blocks other processes. The cyclic nature of this problem can easily manifest itself to different processes locking each other up waiting for the P-SQL to release the locks on the original table. A P-SQL sitting on a table will be recorded on the master..syslogsshold table. For example in the following example, reorg rebuild process has created a long running transaction as recorded in master..syslogsshold. Please note that for every replicated database, there will be an entry in this table as well.

```
1> select * from master..syslogshold
2> go
```

```
dbid    reserved      spid     page           xactid           masterxactid
starttime                      name
xloid
------  -----------   ------   ----------     -------------    --------------   ------
--------------------   --------------------------------------------------------
------------   -----------
    12          0      125        257393 0x71ed03001600 0x000000000000
Oct 20 2004   4:43PM $REORG REBUILD test1 ID=995531599
250
     6          0        0         74315 0x000000000000 0x000000000000
Oct 20 2004   4:39PM $replication_truncation_point
0
```

Locks Held on Different Tables

You can use the following stored procedures (based on an original script
by Ed Barlow [11]) to get the list of the locks held on different tables:

```
use sybsystemprocs
go
create procedure sp__lock( @dbname char(30)=null,@spid smallint=null )
as
begin
declare @dbid smallint
if @dbname is not null
        select @dbid=db_id(@dbname)
if (charindex("sa_role", show_role()) > 0)
begin
                select
                        "Type"=substring(v.name,1,11),
                        "User"=substring(suser_name(p.suid)+"
(pid="+rtrim(convert(char(5),l.spid))+")",1,18),

"Table"=substring(db_name(l.dbid)+".."+convert(char(20),object_name(l.id,l.
dbid)),1,22),
                        "Page"=convert(char(8),l.page),
                        "Cmd"=substring(p.cmd,1,11)
                        from     master..syslocks l,
                                    master..sysprocesses p,
                                    master..spt_values v
                        where      p.spid=l.spid
                              and      l.type = v.number
                              and      v.type = "L"
                              and          p.dbid=isnull(@dbid,p.dbid)
                              and          p.spid=isnull(@spid,p.spid)
                              and          l.dbid=isnull(@dbid,l.dbid)
                              and          l.spid=isnull(@spid,l.spid)
                        order by l.dbid, l.id, v.name
                           return
end
        select
                "Type"=substring(v.name,1,11),
```

```
                        "Usernm"=substring(suser_name(p.suid)+"
(pid="+rtrim(convert(char(5),l.spid))+")",1,18),
                        "TableNm"=convert(char(22),db_name(l.dbid)+".."),
                        "Page"=convert(char(8),l.page),
                        "Cmd"=substring(p.cmd,1,11),
                                        l.id,
                                        l.dbid
        into    #locks
        from     master..syslocks l,
                                master..sysprocesses p,
                                master..spt_values v
        where    p.spid=l.spid
                and    l.type = v.number
                and    v.type = "L"
                and                l.dbid=isnull(@dbid,l.dbid)
                and                l.spid=isnull(@spid,l.spid)
                and                p.dbid=isnull(@dbid,p.dbid)
                and                p.spid=isnull(@spid,p.spid)
        update #locks
        set     TableNm=TableNm+object_name(id,dbid)
        where dbid=db_id() or dbid=1 or dbid=2
        update #locks
        set     TableNm=TableNm+convert(varchar,id)
        where dbid<>db_id() and dbid>2
        delete #locks
        where TableNm like "tempdb..#locks%"
        select Type, "User"=Usernm, "Table"=TableNm, Page, Cmd
        from #locks
        order by dbid, id, Type
        return 0
end
```

Output from the above store procedure will display something resembling the following:

```
Type          User                Table                     Page      Cmd
----------    ------------------  ------------------------  --------  -----------
Sh_intent     sa (pid=101)        master..spt_values        0         SELECT
Ex_table      zubeza (pid=62)     its_ged_prod..test1       0         UPDATE
Ex_table-bl   vickpa (pid=173)    options..test1            0         DELETE
```

Analyze the SQL running on the Server

We now know how to start and look at the processes running in ASE when we encounter problems. We simply examine the processes running and the locks held by the individual processes on different tables. However we require more information than that. We really need to identify the characteristics of the processes running on ASE, in terms of their

83

CPU, memory and I/O utilization and other interesting parameters. In addition, it is also useful to know the elapsed time for each query.

Top *N* SQL being processed

You can use the stored procedure below to identify top *N* SQL processes being executed in your server. This procedure relies on the following MDA tables:

master..monProcessProcedures
master..monProcessSQLText
master..monProcessActivity

in conjunction with

master..sysprocesses

The sort order used by this stored procedure is by CPU time. However, you can change the sort order to sort on Logical I/O, Physical I/O etc.:

```
use sybsystemprocs
go
drop procedure sp__topn
go
create procedure sp__topn
(
        @spid int = null
)
as
begin
if @spid is not null
begin
select
        suser_name(p.suid)  "Name",
        m.SPID,
        m.DBName,
        m.ObjectName,
        m.MemUsageKB,
        o.CPUTime,
        o.LogicalReads,
        o.PhysicalReads,
        o.PhysicalWrites,
        o.Transactions,
        o.Commits,
        o.Rollbacks,
        o.WaitTime,
        n.SQLText
from master..monProcessProcedures m,
    master..sysprocesses p,
```

```
        master..monProcessSQLText n,
        master..monProcessActivity o
where m.SPID = p.spid
AND    m.SPID = n.SPID
AND    p.spid = n.SPID
AND    p.spid = o.SPID
AND m.SPID=@spid
order by o.CPUTime
end
else
begin
select
        suser_name(p.suid) "Name",
        m.SPID,
        m.DBName,
        m.ObjectName,
        m.MemUsageKB,
        o.CPUTime,
        o.LogicalReads,
        o.PhysicalReads,
        o.PhysicalWrites,
        o.Transactions,
        o.Commits,
        o.Rollbacks,
        o.WaitTime,
        n.SQLText
from master..monProcessProcedures m,
     master..sysprocesses p,
     master..monProcessSQLText n,
     master..monProcessActivity o
where m.SPID = p.spid
AND    m.SPID = n.SPID
AND    p.spid = n.SPID
AND    p.spid = o.SPID
AND    p.spid <> @@spid
order by o.CPUTime
end
end
go
```

An output from this query will resemble the following for the above processes:

```
Name                               SPID    DBName
ObjectName                         MemUsageKB  CPUTime    LogicalReads
PhysicalReads PhysicalWrites Transactions Commits      Rollbacks   WaitTime
        SQLText
-------------------------------- ------ ------------------------------ -----
-------------------------------- ----------- ----------- ------------ ------------
- -------------- ----------- ----------- ----------- -----------
        --------------------------------------------------------------------
---------------------------------------------------------------------------------
---------------------------------------------------------------------------------
--------------------------------------
```

85

```
 gillia                              76 options
test1_insert_sp                      16        1200      50078115
610         1475295          0    1363571    1363571      4229000
         exec test1_insert_sp 10000000
 alfoka                             146 options
test1_insert_sp                      16        2000      51373493
486         1516152          0    1399329    1399328      4131500
         exec test1_insert_sp 7500000
 zubeza                              62 its_ged_prod
update_process_sp                    36        2200       3274041
1093        1484800          0       9486       9485      2343600
         exec update_process_sp
 vickpa                             173 options
delete_from_test1_sp                 36       23000     18482692
57573         63619          0        445        439       187200
         exec delete_from_test1_sp
```

The output displays among other things Memory usage, CPU time and the SQL text for each SQL statement. In addition, the numbers of transactions commits and rollbacks are also shown. The I/O characteristics are also provided for each SQL statement. Here you can see the number of disk reads (physical reads) and cache gets (logical reads) along with the number of disk writes (physical writes). Note that queries that have been executed once may have misleading statistics with respect to disk reads, as the data needed for the first run of the query was likely read in from disk to memory (cache). Therefore, the number of disk reads per execution should drop for subsequent executions and the I/O hit ratio for the query should rise.

The columns of the top *N* result set will provide clues to the repetition metric for the query. When troubleshooting a slow system, you should be on the lookout for any query that shows a higher CPU Time and or Memory Usage that is significantly larger that any other query on the system. It may be that the query is looping, or other problematic programming issue.

In our case by looking at the process 173, you will see that this process has accumulated a total CPU time of order of magnitude higher than other processes although the actual memory usage is quite low. The reason is that this process is being blocked most of the time, waiting for locks to be freed and hence utilizing a lot of CPU time. Also notice the excessive number of physical reads for process 62.

Measure the Elapsed Time for Each Query

In addition, you can use the following stored procedure (a variation of this stored procedure was published in ASE 105 paper in TechWave 2004) to measure the elapsed time for each query

```
use sybsystemprocs
go
create procedure sp__ElapsedTime
as
select
SPID,
ProcName = isnull(object_name(ProcedureID, DBID),"UNKNOWN"),
DBNAME = isnull(db_name(DBID), "UNKNOWN"),
ElapsedTime = datediff(ms, min(StartTime), max(EndTime))
into #performance
from master..monSysStatement m
where db_name(DBID) != 'sybsystemprocs'
group by SPID, DBID, ProcedureID, BatchID
having ProcedureID != 0
order by 3
select
"Name" = substring(suser_name(p.suid),1,20),
SPID,
"Procedure" = ProcName,
"Database" = DBNAME,
"Elapsed Time/ms" = ElapsedTime
from #performance t,
master..sysprocesses p
where t.SPID = p.spid
and ElapsedTime > 0
order by ElapsedTime
go
```

Providing the following output:

Name Elapsed Time/ms	SPID	Procedure	Database
vickpa 26800	173	delete_from_test1_sp	options
alfoka 65793	146	test1_insert_sp	options
alfoka 65796	146	get_next_rowid_sp	options
gillia 68776	76	test1_insert_sp	options
gillia 68776	76	get_next_rowid_sp	options
zubeza 74183	62	update_process_sp	its_ged_prod

Now let us see who is in the system

```
spid    status         loginame      hostname     blk  blk_sec  program
host_prc  dbname                      cmd                cpu       io          tran_name
------  ------------   -----------   ----------   ----  --------  -----------------
--------  --------------------      ----------------  --------  --------  -----------
------
      134 running        sa            linux        0    0             isql
26007     master                      SELECT             0         1
      173 running        vickpa        linux        0    0             isql
25028     options                     DELETE             22        60
$user_transactio
       76 lock sleep     gillia        linux        173  0             isql
1483      options                     INSERT             3         0
       62 running        zubeza        linux        0    0             isql
1590      its_ged_prod                UPDATE             4         0
$user_transactio
      146 lock sleep     alfoka        linux        173  0             isql
1549      options                     INSERT             5         0
```

Note that both processes 76 and 146 are attempting to insert into table
test1, are blocked by process 173 which is deleting records from that
table. A blocked process will almost always yield a longer Elapsed time as
shown in the output above.

Identifying Table and Index Usage

MDA tables allow you to identify the most heavily used tables and indexes
in a database. By doing so we identify DML activities on ASE 15 and
possibly compare the same with those from ASE 12.5. We can do various
analyses on tables and indexes using the following code:

```
--
-- Description: Table & Index analysis usage by table scans, DML activity
etc
--
-- Mich Talebzadeh 2006, ASE 12.5.n
-- |12/02/09| Modified to cater for ASE 15.x
--
set nocount on
--
-- First of all work out the table rows and sizes (reserved)
--
select
        Owner = user_name(o.uid),
        name = o.name,
        tabid = i.id,
        iname = i.name,
        indid = i.indid,
```

```
          low = d.low,
          rowtotal = convert(numeric(18,0), 0),
          reserved = convert(numeric(20, 9), 0),
          data = convert(numeric(20, 9), 0),
          index_size = convert(numeric(20, 9), 0),
          unused = convert(numeric(20, 9), 0)
into #tmp
from sysobjects o, sysindexes i, master.dbo.spt_values d
where i.id = o.id
      and o.id = i.id
      and d.number = 1
      and d.type = "E"
      and o.type = 'U'
/* perform the row counts */
update #tmp
set rowtotal = row_count(db_id(), tabid)
where indid <= 1

/* calculate the counts for indid > 1
-- case of indid = 1, 0 are special cases done later
*/
update #tmp
 set
         reserved = convert(numeric(20, 9),
         reserved_pages(db_id(), tabid, indid)),
         index_size =  convert(numeric(20, 9),
         data_pages(db_id(), tabid, indid)),
         unused = convert(numeric(20, 9),
         ((reserved_pages(db_id(), tabid, indid) -
         (data_pages(db_id(), tabid, indid)))))
where indid > 1

-- calculate for case where indid = 0 */
update #tmp
set
         reserved = convert(numeric(20, 9),
         reserved_pages(db_id(), tabid, indid)),
         data = convert(numeric(20, 9),
         data_pages(db_id(), tabid, indid)),
         unused = convert(numeric(20, 9),
         ((reserved_pages(db_id(), tabid, indid) -
         (data_pages(db_id(), tabid, indid)))))
where indid = 0

/* handle the case where indid = 1, since we need
** to take care of the data and index pages.
*/
update #tmp
set
         reserved = convert(numeric(20, 9),
                 reserved_pages(db_id(), tabid, 0))
                    + convert(numeric(20, 9),
                    reserved_pages(db_id(), tabid, indid)),
                    index_size = convert(numeric(20, 9),
                             data_pages(db_id(), tabid, indid)),
                    data = convert(numeric(20, 9),
```

```sql
                                          data_pages(db_id(), tabid, 0))
where indid = 1

/* calculate the unused count for indid = 1 case.*/
update #tmp
set
        unused = convert(numeric(20, 9),
        reserved - data - index_size)
where indid = 1

--
-- Get the table itself
--
select distinct
                Owner,
                TableName = name,
                RowTotal = convert(char(15), sum(rowtotal)),
                Reserved = convert(char(15), convert(varchar(11),
                           convert(numeric(11, 0), sum(reserved) *
                           (low / 1024))))
                into #table_size
                from #tmp
                group by Owner,name
--
-- Get index details
--
select
                Owner,
                TableName = substring(name,1,30),
                IndexName = substring(iname,1,30),
                "reserved" = convert(char(10), convert(varchar(11),
                           convert(numeric(11, 0),
                                    index_size / 1024 * low)))
into #t1
from #tmp
where indid > 0

-- Identify tables accessed with a table scan
  SELECT
  "Owner" = user_name(o.uid),
  "TableName" = o.name,
  "LogicalReads" = m.LogicalReads,
  "PagesRead" = m.PagesRead,
  "WhenLastUsed" = m.LastUsedDate,
  "Used" = m.UsedCount
  INTO
      #tabscan
  from
      sysobjects o,
      master..monOpenObjectActivity m
  where
      o.type = 'U'
      and o.id = m.ObjectID
      and m.IndexID = 0
      and m.DBID = db_id()
      and object_name(m.ObjectID, m.DBID) not like 'sa_%'
      and object_name(m.ObjectID, m.DBID) not like '%__sa%'
```

```
            and object_name(m.ObjectID, m.DBID) not like 'rs_%'
            and m.UsedCount > 0
print ""
print 'Tables accessed with Table scans ONLY, no index usage'
print ""
    SELECT
        "TableName" = substring(t.Owner+"."+t.TableName, 1, 30),
        "Rows" = convert(numeric(10,0),s.RowTotal),
        "Size/KB" = convert(numeric(10,0),s.Reserved),
        "LogicalReads" = t.LogicalReads,
        "PagesRead" = t.PagesRead,
        "Table scanned" = str(t.Used, 8, 0),
        "When last table scanned" = t.WhenLastUsed
    FROM
        #tabscan t,
        #table_size s
    WHERE
        t.Owner = s.Owner
        and t.TableName = s.TableName
        and not exists (select 1 from master..monOpenObjectActivity m
                        where object_name(m.ObjectID, m.DBID) = t.TableName
                        and object_name(m.ObjectID, m.DBID) =
s.TableName
                        and m.DBID = db_id()
                        and m.IndexID > 0
                        and m.LastUsedDate is not NULL)
    ORDER BY
        t.Owner,
        t.TableName
--
-- Identify tables with no DML
--
    SELECT
    "Owner" = user_name(o.uid),
    "TableName" = o.name,
    "LogicalReads" = m.LogicalReads,
    "LockRequests" = m.LockRequests,
    "Operations" = m.Operations,
    "Selected" = m.OptSelectCount,
    "WhenLastSelected" = m.LastOptSelectDate,
    "Used" = m.UsedCount,
    "WhenLastUsed" = m.LastUsedDate
    INTO
        #dormant
    from
        sysobjects o,
        master..monOpenObjectActivity m
    where
        object_name(m.ObjectID, m.DBID) = o.name
        and o.type = 'U'
        and o.id = m.ObjectID
        and m.IndexID = 0  -- Only tables!
        and m.DBID = db_id()
        and object_name(m.ObjectID, m.DBID) not like 'sa_%'
        and object_name(m.ObjectID, m.DBID) not like '%__sa%'
        and object_name(m.ObjectID, m.DBID) not like 'rs_%'
        and m.RowsInserted = 0
```

```
        and m.RowsUpdated = 0
        and m.RowsDeleted = 0
  PRINT ""
  PRINT "Displaying dormant tables with no DML activity, table scan or
index usage"
  PRINT ""
  SELECT
        "TableName" = substring(t.Owner+"."+t.TableName, 1, 30),
        "Rows" = convert(numeric(10,0),s.RowTotal),
        "Size/KB" = convert(numeric(10,0),s.Reserved),
        "LogicalReads" = t.LogicalReads,
        "LockRequests" = t.LockRequests
  FROM
        #dormant t,
        #table_size s
  WHERE
        t.Owner = s.Owner
        and t.TableName = s.TableName
        and t.WhenLastUsed is NULL    -- table has never been used by the
optimiser
        -- and no index of this table has been used by the optimiser
        and not exists (select 1 from master..monOpenObjectActivity m
                        where object_name(m.ObjectID, m.DBID) = t.TableName
                             and object_name(m.ObjectID, m.DBID) =
s.TableName
                             and m.DBID = db_id()
                             and m.IndexID > 0
                             and m.LastUsedDate is not NULL)
  ORDER BY
        t.Owner,
        t.TableName
--
-- Identify tables with DML activity
--
  SELECT
  "Owner" = user_name(o.uid),
  "TableName" = o.name,
  "LogicalReads" = m.LogicalReads,
  "LockRequests" = m.LockRequests,
  "Operations" = m.Operations,
  "Selected" = m.OptSelectCount,
  "WhenLastSelected" = m.LastOptSelectDate,
  "Used" = m.UsedCount,
  "WhenLastUsed" = m.LastUsedDate,
  "Inserted" = m.RowsInserted,
  "Updated" = m.RowsUpdated,
  "Deleted" = m.RowsDeleted
  INTO
        #temp
  from
        sysobjects o,
        master..monOpenObjectActivity m
  where
        object_name(m.ObjectID, m.DBID) = o.name
        and o.type = 'U'
        and o.id = m.ObjectID
        and m.IndexID = 0
```

```
              and m.DBID = db_id()
          and object_name(m.ObjectID, m.DBID) not like 'sa_%'
          and object_name(m.ObjectID, m.DBID) not like '%__sa%'
          and object_name(m.ObjectID, m.DBID) not like 'rs_%'
          and (m.RowsInserted > 0 or m.RowsUpdated > 0 or  m.RowsDeleted > 0)
SELECT
"TableName" = object_name(m.ObjectID, m.DBID),
"IndexName" = i.name,
"Selected" = m.OptSelectCount,
"WhenLastSelected" = m.LastOptSelectDate,
"Used" = m.UsedCount,
"WhenLastUsed" = m.LastUsedDate
into #used
from master..monOpenObjectActivity m,
sysindexes i
where
    m.IndexID > 0
and m.IndexID <> 255 -- ignore text, image data chain
and m.IndexID = i.indid
and m.ObjectID = i.id
and m.DBID = db_id()
print ""
if exists(select 1 from #used where Selected = 0 and Used = 0)
begin
  print ""
  print 'Indexes never selected or used by the optimizer'
  print ""
  select
          "TableName" = substring(i.Owner+"."+i.TableName, 1, 30),
          "IndexName" = substring(u.IndexName,1,30),
          "IndexSize/KB" = i.reserved,
          u.Selected,
          u.Used
  from   #used u,
         #t1 i
  where u.TableName = i.TableName
        and u.IndexName = i.IndexName
        and u.Selected = 0 and u.Used = 0
  order by u.TableName,
          u.IndexName
end
if exists(select 1 from #used where Selected > 0 and Used = 0)
begin
  print ""
  print 'Indexes selected by the optimizer but never used in query'
  print ""
  select
        "TableName" = substring(i.Owner+"."+i.TableName, 1, 30),
        "IndexName" = substring(u.IndexName,1,30),
        "IndexSize/KB" = i.reserved,
        u.Selected,
        "When Last selected" = u.WhenLastSelected
  from   #used u,
         #t1 i
  where u.TableName = i.TableName
        and u.IndexName = i.IndexName
        and u.Selected > 0 and u.Used = 0
```

```
      order by u.TableName,
               u.IndexName
end
if exists(select 1 from #used where Selected = 0 and Used > 0)
begin
  print ""
  print 'Indexes Used by the optimizer but never selected'
  print ""
  select
          "TableName" = substring(i.Owner+"."+i.TableName, 1, 30),
          "IndexName" = substring(u.IndexName,1,30),
          "IndexSize/KB" = i.reserved,
          u.Selected
  from    #used u,
          #t1 i
  where   u.TableName = i.TableName
          and u.IndexName = i.IndexName
          and u.Selected = 0 and u.Used > 0
  order by u.TableName,
           u.IndexName
end
PRINT ""
PRINT "Displaying tables with DML activity"
PRINT ""
SELECT
        "TableName" = substring(t.Owner+"."+t.TableName, 1, 30),
        "Rows" = convert(numeric(10,0),s.RowTotal),
        "Size/KB" = convert(numeric(10,0),s.Reserved),
        t.Inserted,
        t.Updated,
        t.Deleted,
        t.LockRequests,
        "SUM DML ACTIVITY/ROWS " =
        CASE
           WHEN t.Inserted+t.Updated+t.Deleted > 0 and
convert(numeric(10,0),s.RowTotal) > 0
              THEN
convert(varchar(9),(t.Inserted+t.Updated+t.Deleted)/convert(numeric(10,
0),s.RowTotal))
           WHEN t.Inserted+t.Updated+t.Deleted > 0 and
convert(numeric(10,0),s.RowTotal) = 0
              THEN " ==> Update stats advisable"
        END
FROM
        #temp t,
        #table_size s
WHERE
        t.Owner = s.Owner
        and t.TableName = s.TableName
ORDER BY
        t.Owner,
        t.TableName
--
-- work out sum of index usage for tables where index(s) have been used
--
SELECT  TableName,
        SumUsed =sum(Used)
```

94

```
into    #sumused
from    #used
where   Used > 0
group by TableName
print ""
select  TableName,
        IndexName,
        Selected,
        Used,
        WhenLastUsed
into    #clean
from    #used
where   Used > 0
print ""
print 'Tables accessed with Table scans and index usage as well'
print ""
  SELECT
        "TableName" = substring(t.Owner+"."+t.TableName, 1, 30),
        "Rows" = convert(numeric(10,0),s.RowTotal),
        "Size/KB" = convert(numeric(10,0),s.Reserved),
        "LogicalReads" = t.LogicalReads,
        "PagesRead" = t.PagesRead,
        "Table Scans" = str(t.Used, 8, 0),
        "Index Usage" = str(u.SumUsed, 8, 0),
          "IndexUsage/TableScan" = str(u.SumUsed*1.0/t.Used*1.0, 9, 2)
  FROM
        #tabscan t,
        #table_size s,
        #sumused u
  WHERE
        t.Owner = s.Owner
        and t.TableName = s.TableName
        and t.TableName = u.TableName
        and s.TableName = u.TableName
        and u.SumUsed > 0
  ORDER BY
        t.Owner,
        t.TableName
--
SELECT  TableName,
        IndexName,
        Selected,
        Used,
        "Selected_over_sum_selected" =
convert(numeric(10,2),Selected*1.0/sum(Selected)*1.0),
        "Used_over_sum_used" =
convert(numeric(10,2),Used*1.0/sum(Used)*1.0),
        "Used_over_selected" = convert(numeric(10,2),Used*1.0/Selected*1.0)
into #results
from #clean
group by TableName

if exists (select 1 from #results)
begin
  print ""
  print 'Index usage analysis'
  print ""
```

```
select
      "TableName" = substring(i.Owner+"."+i.TableName, 1, 30),
      "IndexName" = substring(r.IndexName,1,30),
      "IndexSize/KB" = i.reserved,
      r.Selected,
      r.Used,
      --"Selected/SUM(Selected)" = r.Selected_over_sum_selected,
      "Used/SUM(Used)" = convert(numeric(10,2),r.Used_over_sum_used)
      --"Used/Selected" = r.Used_over_selected
  from   #results r,
         #t1 i
  where
         r.TableName = i.TableName
         and  r.IndexName = i.IndexName
         --and r.Used_over_sum_used < 1.0
  order by r.TableName, r.Used_over_sum_used desc
end
```

A typical output from this query will look like the following:

```
Tables accessed with Table scans ONLY, no index usage

 TableName                        Rows          Size/KB       LogicalReads
PagesRead    Table scanned When last table scanned
 ------------------------------ ------------- ------------- ------------ --
--------- ------------- -------------------------
 dbo.t_benchmark                               340            384
780          511        454          May 19 2009  2:50PM
   dbo.t_issuer_sector                         19212          3984
79477        437     34225              Jun 25 2009  5:21PM

Displaying dormant tables with no DML activity, table scan or index usage

 TableName                        Rows          Size/KB       LogicalReads
LockRequests
 ------------------------------ ------------- ------------- ------------ --
----------
 dbo.t_aggregate_holding            1023690        270060
546626       805537
 dbo.t_archive_date                     0            64
38         109


Indexes never selected or used by the optimizer

 TableName                        IndexName                     IndexSize/KB
Selected     Used
 ---------------------------- ----------------------------- -------------
----------- -----------
 dbo.t_aggregate_holding        ncl_instrument_id
90020         0                0
 dbo.t_archive_date             pk_archive_date
64         0                0

Indexes selected by the optimizer but never used in query
```

96

```
TableName                        IndexName                          IndexSize/KB
Selected      When Last selected
--------------------------       ------------------------------     ------------
----------- -------------------------
  dbo.t_benchmark                      pk_t_benchmark
192          4       May 19 2009  2:50PM
  dbo.t_benchmark_type                 pk_t_benchmark_type
128          4       May 19 2009  2:50PM

Displaying tables with DML activity

TableName                        Rows          Size/KB        Inserted
Updated      Deleted      LockRequests SUM DML ACTIVITY/ROWS
-----------------------------    -------------- -------------- ----------- ---
-------- ----------- ------------   -------------------------
  dbo.t_instrument                    373404          165952
0        10300              0       10438 0.0275840
  dbo.t_instrument_alt_code         1232424          768800
40320            0         40318    134544 0.0654304

Tables accessed with Table scans and index usage as well

TableName                        Rows          Size/KB        LogicalReads
PagesRead    Table Scans Index Usage IndexUsage/TableScan
-----------------------------    -------------- -------------- ------------ --
--------- ----------- ----------- --------------------
dbo.ICRSHoldingDataImport            10288           6944
1717454529     209252     2524       218       0.09
  dbo.IndexImport                     1173            538
776373109      1899      14853       3670      0.25

Index usage analysis

TableName                        IndexName                          IndexSize/KB
Selected     Used         Used/SUM(Used)
-----------------------------    ------------------------------     ------------
----------- ----------- ---------------
  dbo.t_fund                         index_01
372          4           222           1.00
  dbo.t_instrument_alt_code          index_01
192200          11       121758        0.56
```

The points to watch or used as indicators of potential issues in upgrade are:

- Is a table showing excessive table scan
- Are there indexes that are never used or used with far less frequency compared to ASE 12.5
- Is there an order of magnitude differences in some index usage in ASE 15 compared with those of ASE 12.5. What is the underlying reason for that? Index usage is obviously a welcome sign. However, excessive index usage can mask potential issues with subqueries.

The code might perform badly if the subquery has to be evaluated many times for different parent query block correlation values!

- If certain tables in ASE 12.5 are used but not in ASE 15, these generally indicate missing applications that have not been considered in ASE 15. For example, there may be certain archive tables that are only used for month-end processing in PROD but omitted in ASE 15 tests.

Working out device hit statistics

We mentioned about big devices in ASE 15. It is advisable to check the hit pattern of ASE devices to ensure that ASE 15 devices are getting the correct throughput. The assumption is that these devices in terms of service time etc should be as good as the devices on ASE 15. For example, if you have switched to file systems as opposed to raw partitions, the assumptions would be that you expect on par or better matrix on these new devices compared to ASE 15. In the stored procedure below, the readings are based on the MDA table *master..monDeviceIO*. The following should be noted:

- Reads include non-APFReads and APFReads
- Large amount of APFReads usually point to table scans!
- svc_t or service time is the average service time for IO requests in ms
- Any svc_t outside of 2-8 ms should be considered slow
- The sampling interval. The statistics tend to be more accurate for device hits > 50,000 IOs
- Slow device in Notes column indicates Total IOs > 50,000 and average service time > 8 ms

```
CREATE PROC sp__devhits(
                @num_unit_delay int=NULL,      -- sample time
                @num_iter int=NULL,            -- sample iteration
                @unit char(1)=NULL )           -- Unit of sample hour,
minute or second
AS
/*************************************************************************
****
**
** Name        : sp__devhits
**
** Created By  : Mich Talebzadeh based on sp__monio proc by Ed Barlow (GEM
LIbrary)
** Date        : 16/03/2009
```

```
**  Purpose      : Works out various device IO matrix from monDeviceIO
**                You can specify the unit of sampling interval in S (1-59,
seconds), M (1-59, minutes) or H (1-99 hours)
**
**                Examples.
**                Do 9 hours, 1 iteration of disk IO matrix
**                exec sp__devhits 9,1,h
**                Do  5 iterations of 50 seconds sampling
**                exec sp__devhits 50,5,s
**
****************************************************************************
***/
set nocount on
declare @delay char(8)
/*
** Compute number of Pages in a Megabyte.
*/
declare @low     int, @pgsmb float        /* Number of Pages per Megabytes */

select @pgsmb = (1048576. / v.low) from   master.dbo.spt_values v
where v.number = 1 and    v.type = "E"


select
        name
        ,"SizeMB" = convert(char(6),convert(int,((1. + high -
low)/@pgsmb)))
into #devsize
from master..sysdevices

if @unit is not null
begin
    if UPPER(@unit) not in ('S','M','H')
    begin
        print 'The unit has to be in S (seconds), M (minutes) or H (hours)'
        return -1
    end
    else
      begin
        set @unit = UPPER(@unit)
        if(@unit = 'H' and @num_unit_delay < 10) set
@delay=convert(char(1),@num_unit_delay)+":00:00"
        if(@unit = 'H' and @num_unit_delay >= 10) set
@delay=convert(char(2),@num_unit_delay)+":00:00"
        if(@unit = 'H' and @num_unit_delay > 99) return -1
        if(@unit = 'M' and @num_unit_delay < 10) set
@delay="00:"+convert(char(1),@num_unit_delay)+":00"
        if(@unit = 'M' and @num_unit_delay >= 10) set
@delay="00:"+convert(char(2),@num_unit_delay)+":00"
        if(@unit = 'M' and @num_unit_delay > 99) return -1
        if(@unit = 'S' and @num_unit_delay < 10) set @delay
="00:00:0"+convert(char(1),@num_unit_delay)
        if(@unit = 'S' and @num_unit_delay >= 10) set
@delay="00:00:"+convert(char(2),@num_unit_delay)
        if(@unit = 'S' and @num_unit_delay >= 60) return - 1
      end
end
```

```
declare @date datetime, @longunit char(7)

if @num_unit_delay is null
begin
        set @date = getdate()
        print " Starting at %1!",@date
        print " "
        select
                "Device (size)" = substring(m.LogicalName+" ("+d.SizeMB+"
MB)",1,30)
                ,m.Reads
                ,m.APFReads
                ,m.Writes
                ,"Total IOs" = m.Reads+m.Writes
                ,"Total IOTime/ms" = m.IOTime
                ,"svc_t/ms" =
convert(numeric(10,1),(IOTime*1.0)/(Reads+Writes)*1.)
        from   master..monDeviceIO m, #devsize d
        where  m.LogicalName = d.name
        order by (m.Reads+m.Writes)*1./(m.IOTime*1.0)
end
else
begin
        select
                 LogicalName
                ,Reads
                ,APFReads
                ,Writes
                ,IOTime
        into #tmp
        from   master..monDeviceIO

        if @num_iter is null
                select @num_iter=100
        while @num_iter>0
        begin
                set @date = getdate()
                if @unit = 'H' set @longunit = 'hours'
                if @unit = 'M' set @longunit = 'minutes'
                if @unit = 'S' set @longunit = 'seconds'
                print " %1!, waiting for %2! %3! to collect
statistics",@date,@num_unit_delay,@longunit
                print " "
                waitfor delay @delay

                print ""
                print "Below IOTime is Total amount of time (in
milliseconds) spent waiting for IO requests to be satisfied"
                print "Reads include non-APFReads and APFReads"
                print "Large amount of APFReads usually point to table
scans!"
                print "svc_t or service time is the average service time
for IO requests in ms"
                print "Any svc_t outside of 2-8 ms should be considered
slow"
                print "The sampling interval. The statistics tend to be
more accurate for device hits > 50,000 IOs"
```

```
                print "Slow device in Notes column below indicates Total
IOs > 50,000 and average service time > 8 ms"
                print "Devices incurring IOTime"
                print ""
                select
                                "Device (size)" =
substring(m.LogicalName+" ("+d.SizeMB+" MB)",1,30)
                                ,Reads= m.Reads-t.Reads
                                ,APFReads=           m.APFReads-t.APFReads
                                ,Writes=             m.Writes-t.Writes
                                ,"Total IOs" = (m.Reads-t.Reads)+(m.Writes-
t.Writes)
                                ,"IOTime/ms" =  m.IOTime-t.IOTime
                                ,"svc_t/ms" =
                                CASE when m.IOTime-t.IOTime > 0
                                  THEN
                                                convert(numeric(10,1),
                                  ((m.IOTime-t.IOTime)*1.0)/((m.Reads-
t.Reads)+(m.Writes-t.Writes))*1.)
                                ELSE
                                                0
                                END
                                ,"Notes" =
                                CASE when
                                        -- > 50,000 IOs aqnd srvice time > 8
ms
                                        ((m.Reads-t.Reads)+(m.Writes-
t.Writes)) > 50000
                                        and (((m.IOTime-
t.IOTime)*1.0)/((m.Reads-t.Reads)+(m.Writes-t.Writes))*1.) > 8.0
                                  THEN
                                                "Slow device"
                                ELSE
                                                ""
                                END
                from master..monDeviceIO m,#tmp t, #devsize d
                where
                m.LogicalName = t.LogicalName
                and
                m.LogicalName = d.name
                and m.IOTime-t.IOTime > 0
                order by ((m.Reads-t.Reads)+(m.Writes-
t.Writes))*1./((m.IOTime-t.IOTime)*1.0)

                print ""
                print "Devices incurring no IOTime or inactive"
                select
                                "Device (size)" =
substring(m.LogicalName+" ("+d.SizeMB+" MB)",1,30)
                                ,Reads= m.Reads-t.Reads
                                ,APFReads=           m.APFReads-t.APFReads
                                ,Writes=             m.Writes-t.Writes
                                ,"Total IOs" = (m.Reads-t.Reads)+(m.Writes-
t.Writes)
                                ,"IOTime/ms" =  m.IOTime-t.IOTime
                                ,"svc_t/ms" = 0
                from master..monDeviceIO m,#tmp t, #devsize d
```

101

```
                where
                m.LogicalName = t.LogicalName
                and
                m.LogicalName = d.name
                and m.IOTime-t.IOTime = 0
                order by m.LogicalName

                delete #tmp

                insert #tmp
                select LogicalName,Reads,APFReads,Writes,IOTime
                from    master..monDeviceIO

                select @num_iter = @num_iter - 1
        end
end

return


1>  sp__devhits 9,1,h
2> go
 Mar 18 2009  9:06PM, waiting for 9 H to collect statistics
Below IOTime is Total amount of time (in milliseconds) spent waiting for IO
requests to be satisfied
Reads include non-APFReads and APFReads
Large amount of APFReads usually point to table scans!
svc_t or service time is the average service time for IO requests in ms
Any svc_t outside of 2-8 ms should be considered slow
The sampling interval. The statistics tend to be more accurate for device
hits > 50,000 IOs
Slow device in Notes column indicates Total IOs > 50,000 and average
service time > 8 ms
Devices incurring IOTime
 Device (size)                         Reads      APFReads    Writes      Total
IOs    IOTime/ms    svc_t/ms       Notes
 ------------------------------------- ----------- ----------- ----------- -------
---- ----------- -------------- -----------
 tempdevcb (500 MB)                      1715          0         133451
135166    40699000           301.1 Slow device
 datadev7 (5120 MB)                     25614        4512        93967
119581    1404400            11.7 Slow device
 sysprocsdev (200 MB)                     11           0
8         19          200       10.5
 datadev3 (5120 MB)                    172110        6749       426859
598969    6155400            10.2 Slow device
 datadev1 (5120 MB)                    159317       25010       135283
```

102

```
294600      2615500               8.8 Slow device
  tempdevce (500 MB)                       71          0         23669
23740       173300            7.2
  datadev2 (5120 MB)                   156897      16297        320838
477735      2876400           6.0
  datadev16 (24000 MB)                  61272      33131        102776
164048      898900            5.4
Devices incurring no IOTime or inactive
 Device (size)                   Reads    APFReads    Writes    Total
 IOs    IOTime/ms   svc_t/ms
-------------------------------  ---------- ----------- ----------- -------
---- ----------- -----------
 tempdb_fmw_log1 (250 MB)                   0          0
0          0           0          0
 tempdb_fmw_log2 (250 MB)                   0          0
0          0           0          0
```

Code freeze before go live

It is prudent that some form of code freeze is implemented before going live. This code freeze should affect all the databases that will be going through the upgrade process in a phased migration or all databases. The thinking behind this approach is to ensure that Monday after going live you deal with as little surprises as possible. We all know the perils of putting somehow defective code into PROD (defective meaning not completely tested impacting production results or performance) and promoting retrofits in a hurry. Although this is a known scenario, the last thing you want in upgrade is releasing code at the last minute. If the code turns up to be defective, you will struggle to determine whether the code is defective or ASE 15 is the culprit. My recommendation is that a two-week code freeze (bar emergency fixes) should be applied to PROD prior to going live to minimise any systematic uncertainties.

Making sense of the optimizer output

I added this section because I felt that one cannot upgrade ASE 15 without appreciating the way the new optimizer works. Admittedly this section may not be fully the DBA responsibility but it is assumed that like any other performance issues, inputs from both developers and DBAs are required. In other words at some point the performance issues with the code will be thrown at the DBA. I start with a brief introduction to the optimizer concepts.

Logical Operators, Physical Operators and the Lava Execution Engine

Before going into ins and outs of ASE 15 optimizer, we need to get familiar with the concepts. *Parser and Pre-processing* convert the user query into *Logical operator (Lop) tree*. Lop tree is the input into the optimizer whose output is a *Physical operator (Pop) tree*. Operators describe how the optimizer executes a query. The optimizer uses operators to build a query plan to create the result specified in the query

Logical operators as the names sound describe relational query processing operation on a conceptual level. On the other hand, Physical operators actually implement the operation defined by a logical operator, using a concrete method or algorithm. For example, *join* is a logical operation, whereas *nested loop join*, *hash join* or *sort merge join* are examples of physical operators.

Physical operators are classed as *primitive operations*. All primitive operations have an output: their *result set*. Each input of primitive operation should be connected to the output of another primitive operation. That is why an execution plan can be sketched as a *tree*.

The optimizer accepts a query as a tree consisting of logical operators. The optimizer then chooses the most efficient physical operator plan for the query. The optimizer uses a costing model to determine which physical operator will implement a logical operator and the join order etc. Usually, a logical operation can be implemented by multiple physical operators. For example, Lop of *join* type can be implemented using *NLJ* or *MJ* etc and the optimizer will consider these alternative physical models in its plan.

Whatever we have discussed so far applies more and less to the optimization techniques in relational databases. However, what distinguishes one engine from another is the implementation technique chosen for query execution.

104

The next step after the Physical Operator (Pop) tree is to get the tree ready for the **Query Execution Engine**. ASE 15 uses **Lava operators** for this purpose and calls this engine **Lava Execution Engine**. In summary, the Pop tree chosen by the optimizer is compiled into **Lava Query Plans**. In other words, Lava operators are the implementation of physical operators in the Lava Execution Engine. A Lava Query Plan is built as an upside down tree of Lava Operators as we shall see shortly. *During execution,* control flows from root to the leaves. Each parent lava operator asks for the next row from its child operator(s), when needed.

So in summary, it is useful to remember that during the life of a query in ASE, it roughly goes from a LOP tree to a POP tree and ends up as a LAVA operator tree.

 Not all query plans are compiled into Lava type Query Plans. SQL statements that are not optimizable such as CREATE table, EXECUTE Stored Procedure, DECLARE CURSOR etc are compiled into query plans like those in prior version of ASE and are not executed by the Lava Execution Engine. These plans are either executed by the Procedural Execution Engine or by Utility modules called by the Procedural Engine.

Queries in ASE 15

I have chosen two simple examples to illustrate ASE 15 query processing. Let us start with a query that should use an index scan. The cost of a query for me and you is the measure of time to completion. The major portion of costing comes from the physical and logical I/O that needs to be performed to fetch the data from the disk or memory as the case may be. This shows up clearly when we examine a base table with a single index on it.

Before going further let us prepare ourselves for this simple example:

- There is a base table
- There is a composite index (an index with more than one column) on this table

- We expect the optimizer to use the index to fetch from the table
- Our query has one or more predicates on some of the columns that the index is built on
- Index is crucial for this example. Optimizer uses the index to fetch the results. It may or may not decide to visit the table itself.

Example of a simple selectivity

Let me start by creating a simple table. I have chosen this table to help us understand the index usage and the optimizer output in ASE 15:

```
create table T1 (
            n1                  tinyint                 NOT
NULL,
            ind_pad             varchar(40)             NOT
NULL,
            n2                  tinyint                 NOT
NULL,
            small_vc            varchar(10)             NOT
NULL,
            padding             varchar(200)            NOT
NULL
)
lock datarows
go
create index T1_I1 on T1(n1,ind_pad, n2)
go
```

We made it a DOL table. I will be populating column *n1* with random numbers between 0 to 24. *n2* will be another random number between 0 to19. The column *ind_pad* will be populated with 'x'+space(38)+'x', (40 characters in total) for all rows. Similarly the column *padding* will be 'x'+space(198)+'x' or 200 characters. I have used the columns with padding intentionally to give a meaningful length to the row.

The column *small_vc* is required to be a monolithically increasing number (@number) in character format, starting from 1. You may have noticed that it is a varchar(10). It requires to be padded with leading zeros. In summary a format similar to the one described below:

```
right(replicate("0",10) + convert(varchar,@number), 10)
```

I will use the following algorithm to populate T1 table

```
    INSERT T1
    (
      n1,
      ind_pad,
      n2,
      small_vc,
      padding
    )
    VALUES
    (
      convert(tinyint,rand()*25.0),
      'x'+space(38)+'x',
      convert(tinyint,rand()*20.0),
      right(replicate("0",10) + convert(varchar,@number), 10),
      'x'+space(198)+'x'
    )
```

In the above statement @number is the monolithically incrementing number as discussed. I populate this table with **100,000 records**. The first 10 records are displayed below:

```
n1   ind_pad                                            n2   small_vc   padding
---  -----------------------------------------------    ---  ---------- --------------
------------------------------------------------------------------------------------
------------------------------------------------------------------------------------
------------------------------------------
  12 x                                                  x    7 0000000001 x
x
   8 x                                                  x    3 0000000002 x
x
  23 x                                                  x   12 0000000003 x
x
  13 x                                                  x    7 0000000004 x
x
   8 x                                                  x    1 0000000005 x
x
  20 x                                                  x    5 0000000006 x
x
  21 x                                                  x   16 0000000007 x
x
  18 x                                                  x    0 0000000008 x
x
   2 x                                                  x   15 0000000009 x
x
  10 x                                                  x    0 0000000010 x
x
```

```
(10 rows affected)
```

Optdiag Output

We created the table, populated it and ran *update index statistics* on the table to bring the statistics for table and index columns up-to-date. Following that, I ran an optdiag to get the information that we require and will use it as a reference henceforth

 Let me bore you with a bit of optdiag and its output. To start with in any ASE database *systabstats* table stores stats about the table or index as an object, that is, the size, number of rows, and so forth. It is updated by query processing, data definition language, and *update statistics* commands. On the other hand, *sysstatistics* table stores information about the values in a specific column. It is updated by data definition language and *update statistics* commands.

The *optdiag* utility displays statistics from the systabstats and sysstatistics tables. Optdiag can also be used to update sysstatistics table information. We can use optdiag to display statistics for an entire database, for a single table and its indexes and columns, or for a particular column. Histograms are created when update statistics command is executed. Optdiag utility can be used to display summary data about histograms. Histogram output is printed in columns.

```
Table name:                          "T1"

Statistics for table:                "T1"

    Data page count:                 14286
    Empty data page count:           0
    Data row count:                  100000.0000000000000000
    Forwarded row count:             0.0000000000000000
    Deleted row count:               0.0000000000000000
    Data page CR count:              1793.0000000000000000
    OAM + allocation page count:     61
    First extent data pages:         0
    Data row size:                   266.0000000000000000
```

108

```
        Parallel join degree:            0.0000000000000000
        Unused page count:               0
        OAM page count:                  1

    Derived statistics:
        Data page cluster ratio:         0.9994400000000000
        Space utilization:               0.9300513290433492
        Large I/O efficiency:            0.9960953063989162

Statistics for index:                    "T1_I1" (nonclustered)
Index column list:                       "n1", "ind_pad", "n2"
        Leaf count:                      513
        Empty leaf page count:           0
        Data page CR count:              98504.0000000000000000
        Index page CR count:             449.0000000000000000
        Data row CR count:               99406.0000000000000000
        First extent leaf pages:         0
        Leaf row size:                   6.4337799999999996
        Index height:                    2

    Derived statistics:
        Data page cluster ratio:         0.0092399098545380
        Index page cluster ratio:        0.1428571428571428
        Data row cluster ratio:          0.0069300231000770
        Space utilization:               0.6264476264476264
        Large I/O efficiency:            0.1428571428571428

Statistics for column:                   "ind_pad"
Last update of column statistics:        Sep 18 2008 10:56:20:026PM

        Range cell density:              0.0000000000000000
        Total density:                   1.0000000000000000
        Range selectivity:               default used (0.33)
        In between selectivity:          default used (0.25)

Histogram for column:                     "ind_pad"
Column datatype:                          varchar(40)
Requested step count:                     20
Actual step count:                        2
Sampling Percent:                         0

        Step      Weight                  Value

          1       0.00000000        <      "x
x"
          2       1.00000000        =      "x
x"

Statistics for column:                    "n1"
Last update of column statistics:         Sep 18 2008 10:56:19:026PM

        Range cell density:              0.0400134694444444
        Total density:                   0.0400112732000000
        Range selectivity:               default used (0.33)
        In between selectivity:          default used (0.25)

Histogram for column:                     "n1"
```

109

```
Column datatype:                        tinyint
Requested step count:                   20
Actual step count:                      20
Sampling Percent:                       0

     Step      Weight                       Value

        1      0.00000000       <           0
        2      0.03951000       =           0
        3      0.08010000       <=          2
        4      0.07962000       <=          4
        5      0.04085000       <           6
        6      0.03982000       =           6
        7      0.08130000       <=          8
        8      0.03970000       <           10
        9      0.03970000       =           10
       10      0.07804000       <=          12
       11      0.04015000       <           14
       12      0.04015000       =           14
       13      0.07934000       <=          16
       14      0.04122000       <           18
       15      0.04105000       =           18
       16      0.07990000       <=          20
       17      0.03975000       <           22
       18      0.03971000       =           22
       19      0.04003000       <           24
       20      0.04006000       =           24

Statistics for column group:            "n1", "ind_pad"
Last update of column statistics:       Sep 18 2008 10:56:19:026PM

     Range cell density:                0.0400134694444444
     Total density:                     0.0400112732000000
     Range selectivity:                 default used (0.33)
     In between selectivity:            default used (0.25)

Statistics for column group:            "n1", "ind_pad", "n2"
Last update of column statistics:       Sep 18 2008 10:56:19:026PM

     Range cell density:                0.0020105525000000
     Total density:                     0.0020101120000000
     Range selectivity:                 default used (0.33)
     In between selectivity:            default used (0.25)

Statistics for column:                   "n2"
Last update of column statistics:       Sep 18 2008 10:56:19:026PM

     Range cell density:                0.0499878984231169
     Total density:                     0.0500137628000000
     Range selectivity:                 default used (0.33)
     In between selectivity:            default used (0.25)

Histogram for column:                    "n2"
Column datatype:                        tinyint
Requested step count:                   20
Actual step count:                      20
Sampling Percent:                       0
```

```
     Step        Weight                        Value

        1       0.00000000        <           0
        2       0.05045000        =           0
        3       0.10156000        <=          2
        4       0.05076000        <           4
        5       0.05049000        =           4
        6       0.04957000        <           6
        7       0.05028000        =           6
        8       0.04877000        <           8
        9       0.05037000        =           8
       10       0.05109000        <          10
       11       0.04900000        =          10
       12       0.04931000        <          12
       13       0.05015000        =          12
       14       0.04872000        <          14
       15       0.04831000        =          14
       16       0.05065000        <          16
       17       0.05043000        =          16
       18       0.04929000        <          18
       19       0.05102000        =          18
       20       0.04978000        <=         19

No statistics for remaining columns:        "padding"
(default values used)                       "small_vc"

Optdiag succeeded.
```

A Basic Query and its showplan Output

Now let us switch on the showplan and do a simple query on this table

```
dbcc traceon(3604) - display to terminal
set showplan on
go
select
        small vc
from
        T1
where   n1 = 2
and     ind pad = 'x'+space(38)+'x'
and     n2      = 3
go
```

In the above simple query, we provided the optimizer with three predicates that make up the INDEX T1.T1_I1. Showplan alone without other *set* parameters displays optimal plan chosen by the optimizer, the access path and the costing (I/O and CPU):

```
QUERY PLAN FOR STATEMENT 1 (at line 1).

1 operator(s) under root


The type of query is SELECT.

ROOT:EMIT Operator

    |SCAN Operator
    |   FROM TABLE
    |   T1
    |   Index : T1_I1
    |   Forward Scan.
    |   Positioning by key.
    |   Keys are:
    |     n1 ASC
    |     ind_pad ASC
    |     n2 ASC
    |   Using I/O Size 2 Kbytes for index leaf pages.
    |   With LRU Buffer Replacement Strategy for index leaf
pages.
    |   Using I/O Size 16 Kbytes for data pages.
    |   With LRU Buffer Replacement Strategy for data pages.


Total estimated I/O cost for statement 1 (at line 1): 5465.
Parse and Compile Time 0.
SQL Server cpu time: 0 ms.
```

For most part, this query plan should be familiar to you. It is basically similar to what you have already seen in pre ASE 15 showplans. However, this showplan now includes additional lava operators. You notice **ROOT: EMIT operator** line at the top. This line appears at the top of every Lava Query Plan (LQP). The *EMIT operator* is the root of the query plan tree and always has one child operator; in our case **SCAN Operator**. The EMIT operator routes the results of the query by sending them to the client or by assigning values from the result row to local variables or to fetch into variables. According to ASE manual [8], the *SCAN Operator* reads rows into the LQP and makes them available for further processing by the other operators in the query plan. This operator can read rows from *cache, list* or *table*.

In this example, we are simply operating on table T1 using the Index T1_I1. The scan direction of the index starts at the first qualifying row. The index scan is performed using 2K I/O size for index leaf pages. The optimizer chose to use 16K buffers to read the base table for the qualified *small_vc* columns. For both the index and table scans, the optimizer chose to use LRU cache replacement strategy. LRU (least recently used) indicates that the data will be brought into memory at the head of the buffer pool (see the diagram below). This is a normal strategy and is an attempt to keep the pages in memory for as long as possible for future use. On the other hand, the fetch-and-discard strategy would be indicated by MRU (most recently used), and it means that the data will be brought into memory near the wash marker of the buffer pool. The data will remain in memory only for a short time because these buffers are frequently overwritten.

 Just to refresh your memory, two cache replacement strategies are used by ASE. These are called *Least Recently Used* (LRU) replacement strategy and *Most Recently Used* (MRU), otherwise known as (fetch-and-discard) replacement strategy" respectively.

LRU is used for:

- Statements that modify data on pages
- Pages that are needed more than once by a single query
- Object Allocation Map pages
- Most index pages
- Any query where LRU strategy is specified

MRU is deployed for table scanning on heaps (i.e. tables with no clustered index). This strategy places pages into the cache just before the wash marker, as shown in the Figure below. Fetch-and-discard is most often used for queries where a page is needed only once by the query. This includes:

- Most table scans in queries that do not use joins
- One or more tables in a join query
- The worktables generated by the query

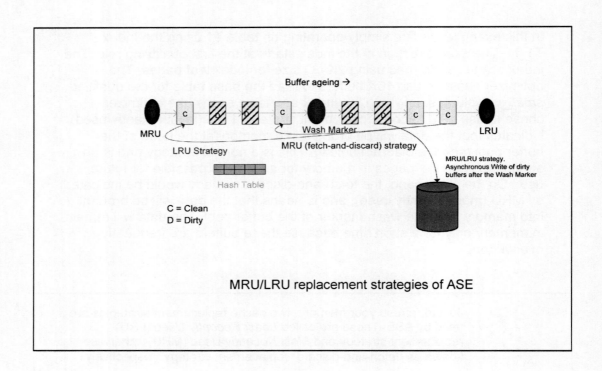

Buffer ageing →

MRU

LRU Strategy

Wash Marker

MRU (fetch-and-discard) strategy

LRU

MRU/LRU strategy.
Asynchronous Write of dirty
buffers after the Wash Marker

Hash Table

C = Clean
D = Dirty

MRU/LRU replacement strategies of ASE

The full plan output

Let us see how the optimizer goes about doing its job in full force. Note the new command *set option show normal* with ASE15 that replaces the trace flags like 302 etc. However, you still need to *set statistics io on* and *set statistics time on* explicitly to get the old execution io and time information (*set option show normal* provides you with the optimizer diagnostics output. There is also a useful new command *set statistics plancost on,* to get the execution time information).

```
dbcc purgesqlcache  -- flush the statement Cache
go
dbcc traceon(3604)
set showplan on
set statistics io on  -- you need this one
set statistics time on -- you need this one
set option show normal
```

114

```
go
select
        small_vc
from
        T1
where   n1 = 2
and     ind_pad = 'x'+space(38)+'x'
and     n2      = 3
```

The output in this run is shown below (I have not shown the results):

```
QUERY PLAN FOR STATEMENT 1 (at line 1).


    STEP 1
        The type of query is EXECUTE.
        Executing a newly cached statement.

Total estimated I/O cost for statement 1 (at line 1): 0.

Parse and Compile Time 0.
SQL Server cpu time: 0 ms.
The Lop tree:
( project
        ( scan T1
        )

)

OptBlock0
        The Lop tree:
        ( scan T1
        )

        Generic Tables: ( Gtt0( T1 ) Gti1( T1_I1 ) )
        Generic Columns: ( Gc0(T1 ,Rid) Gc1(T1 ,n2) Gc2(T1 ,ind_pad)
Gc3(T1 ,n1) Gc4(T1 ,small_vc)) Virtual Generic Columns: ( )
        Predicates: ( { T1.n1 } = 2 tc:{3} { T1.ind_pad } = 'x
x' tc:{2} { T1.n2 } = 3 tc:{1} )
        Transitive Closures: ( Tc0 = { Gc0(T1 ,Rid)} Tc1 = { Gc1(T1 ,n2)}
Tc2 = { Gc2(T1 ,ind_pad)} Tc3 = { Gc3(T1 ,n1)} Tc4 = { Gc4(T1
,small_vc)} )




*************************************************************************
***
        BEGIN: Search Space Traversal for OptBlock0
*************************************************************************
***

Scan plans selected for this optblock:
```

115

```
Beginning selection of qualifying indexes for table 'T1',


Estimating selectivity of index 'T1_I1', indid 2
    n1 = 2
    ind_pad = 'x                                          x'
    n2 = 3
    Estimated selectivity for n1,
        selectivity = 0.04001347,
    Estimated selectivity for ind_pad,
        selectivity = 1,
    Estimated selectivity for n2,
        selectivity = 0.0499879,
    scan selectivity 0.002010552, filter selectivity 0.002010552
    201.0552 rows, 1.027392 pages
    Data Row Cluster Ratio 0.006930023
    Index Page Cluster Ratio 0.09395973
    Data Page Cluster Ratio 0.009434542
    using no index prefetch (size 2K I/O)
    in index cache 'default data cache' (cacheid 0) with LRU replacement

    using table prefetch (size 16K I/O)
    in data cache 'default data cache' (cacheid 0) with LRU replacement
    Data Page LIO for 'T1_I1' on table 'T1' = 200.6619


Estimating selectivity for table 'T1'
    Table scan cost is 100000 rows, 14286 pages,

The table (Datarows) has 100000 rows, 14286 pages,
Data Page Cluster Ratio 1.0000000
    n1 = 2
    Estimated selectivity for n1,
        selectivity = 0.04001347,
    ind_pad = 'x                                          x'
    Estimated selectivity for ind_pad,
        selectivity = 1,
    n2 = 3
    Estimated selectivity for n2,
        selectivity = 0.0499879,
    Search argument selectivity is 0.002010552.
    using table prefetch (size 16K I/O)
    in data cache 'default data cache' (cacheid 0) with LRU replacement
OptBlock0 Eqc{0} -> Pops added:

    ( PopRidJoin ( PopIndScan T1_I1 T1 ) ) cost: [C=5106.045 A=5464.117
1] O(L200.6619,P197.6337,C201.0553) props: [ord:{} Round:1{}]


~~~~~~~~~~~~~~~~~~~~~~~~~~~~~~~~~~~~~~~~~~~~~~~~~~~~~~~~~~~~~~~~~~~~~~~~~~~~~~~~
        BEGIN: APPLYING EXHAUSTIVE SEARCH STRATEGY TO OBTAIN BEST PLAN
~~~~~~~~~~~~~~~~~~~~~~~~~~~~~~~~~~~~~~~~~~~~~~~~~~~~~~~~~~~~~~~~~~~~~~~~~~~~~~~~

~~~~~~~~~~~~~~~~~~~~~~~~~~~~~~~~~~~~~~~~~~~~~~~~~~~~~~~~~~~~~~~~~~~~~~~~~~~~~~~~
        DONE: APPLYING EXHAUSTIVE SEARCH STRATEGY TO OBTAIN BEST PLAN
~~~~~~~~~~~~~~~~~~~~~~~~~~~~~~~~~~~~~~~~~~~~~~~~~~~~~~~~~~~~~~~~~~~~~~~~~~~~~~~~
```

```
The best plan found in OptBlock0 :

( PopRidJoin cost: [C=5106.045 A=5464.117 1]
O(L200.6619,P197.6337,C201.0553) props: [ord:{} Round:1{}] ( PopIndScan
cost: [C=80.91687 A=101.8451 1] O(L3.027392,P3.027392,C201.0553) props:
[ord:{} Round:1{}] Gti1( T1_I1 ) Gtt0( T1 ) ) cost: [C=80.91687 A=101.8451
1] O(L3.027392,P3.027392,C201.0553) props: [ord:{} Round:1{}]
) cost: [C=5106.045 A=5464.117 1] O(L200.6619,P197.6337,C201.0553) props:
[ord:{} Round:1{}]


****************************************************************************
***
          DONE: Search Space Traversal for OptBlock0
****************************************************************************
***

The Abstract Plan (AP) of the final query execution plan:
( i_scan T1_I1 T1 ) ( prop T1 ( parallel 1 ) ( prefetch 2 ) ( lru ) )
To experiment with the optimizer behavior, this AP can be modified and then
passed to the optimizer using the PLAN clause: SELECT/INSERT/DELETE/UPDATE
... PLAN '( ... )
The best global plan (Pop tree) :

PARALLEL:
        number of worker processes = 12
        max parallel degree = 12
        min(configured,set) parallel degree = 12
        min(configured,set) hash scan parallel degree = 12
        max repartition degree = 1
        resource granularity (percentage) = 10


FINAL PLAN ( total cost = 5464.117)
        Path: 5106.045
        Work: 5464.117
        Est: 10570.16
( PopEmit
        proj: {{ T1.small_vc } }
        pred: [Tc{} Pe{}]
        subs: {}
        cost: [
                path: 0
                work: 0
                est: 0
        ]
        I/O estimate : [
                rowcount=201.0552
                averagewidth=17
                pages=1
                lio=0 pio=0 cpu=0
                total lio=0 total pio=0 total cpu=0
        ]
        Cache Strategy: [
                prefetch=YES
                iosize=16384 Bytes
                bufreplace=LRU
```

```
            ]
        order: {}
        part: Round Ptn, Degree(s):[ 1 ], TcId's:[ ]

        ( PopRidJoin
                proj: {{ T1.small_vc } }
                pred: [Tc{} Pe{{ T1.n1 }  = 2,{ T1.ind_pad }  = 'x
x',{ T1.n2 }  = 3}]
                subs: {T1.n2 ,T1.ind_pad ,T1.n1 ,T1.small_vc }
                cost: [
                        path: 5106.045
                        work: 5464.117
                        est: 10570.16
                ]
                I/O estimate : [
                        rowcount=201.0552
                        averagewidth=17
                        pages=200.6619
                        lio=200.6619 pio=197.6337 cpu=201.0552
                        scanlio=0 scanpio=0 scancpu=0
                ]
                Cache Strategy: [
                        prefetch=YES
                        iosize=16384 Bytes
                        bufreplace=LRU
                ]
                order: {}
                part: Round Ptn, Degree(s):[ 1 ], TcId's:[ ]

                ( PopIndScan index: Gti1( T1_I1 )
                            table: Gtt0( T1 )

                        proj: {{ T1.Rid } ,{ T1.n2 } ,{ T1.ind_pad } ,{
T1.n1 } }
                        pred: [Tc{} Pe{{ T1.n1 }  = 2,{ T1.ind_pad }  = 'x
x',{ T1.n2 }  = 3}]
                        subs: {T1.Rid ,T1.n2 ,T1.ind_pad ,T1.n1 }
                        cost: [
                                path: 80.91687
                                work: 101.8451
                                est: 182.762
                        ]
                        I/O estimate : [
                                rowcount=201.0552
                                averagewidth=17
                                pages=1.027392
                                lio=3.027392 pio=3.027392 cpu=201.0552
                                scanlio=0 scanpio=0 scancpu=0
                        ]
                        Cache Strategy: [
                                prefetch=NO
                                iosize=2048 Bytes
                                bufreplace=LRU
                        ]
                        order: {}
                        part: Round Ptn, Degree(s):[ 1 ], TcId's:[ ]
                )
```

```
        )
)

QUERY PLAN FOR STATEMENT 1 (at line 1).

1 operator(s) under root


The type of query is SELECT.

ROOT:EMIT Operator

    |SCAN Operator
    |  FROM TABLE
    |  T1
    |  Index : T1_I1
    |  Forward Scan.
    |  Positioning by key.
    |  Keys are:
    |    n1 ASC
    |    ind_pad ASC
    |    n2 ASC
    |  Using I/O Size 2 Kbytes for index leaf pages.
    |  With LRU Buffer Replacement Strategy for index leaf pages.
    |  Using I/O Size 16 Kbytes for data pages.
    |  With LRU Buffer Replacement Strategy for data pages.


Total estimated I/O cost for statement 1 (at line 1): 5464.
Parse and Compile Time 1.
SQL Server cpu time: 100 ms.

Execution Time 0.
SQL Server cpu time: 0 ms.  SQL Server elapsed time: 0 ms.

(198 rows affected)

Execution Time 0.
SQL Server cpu time: 0 ms.  SQL Server elapsed time: 6 ms.
```

Decrypting the plan Output

OK, this is the boring part. Starting from the top we have

```
QUERY PLAN FOR STATEMENT 1 (at line 1).

    STEP 1
        The type of query is EXECUTE.
        Executing a newly cached statement.
```

```
Total estimated I/O cost for statement 1 (at line 1): 0.

Parse and Compile Time 0.
SQL Server cpu time: 0 ms.
```

Although almost trivial, the important point to note is the fact that I have used *dbcc purgesqlcache* in the code to flush all the SQL statements from the *statement cache* and force the optimizer to construct a new query plan (notice the line *Executing a newly cached statement*).

```
The Lop tree:
( project
        ( scan T1
        )

)
```

The **Lop tree** describes the Logical operator tree here. **Project** refers to an internal reference and sort of design related. I have already described what *Scan T1* means.

```
OptBlock0
        The Lop tree:
        ( scan T1
        )
```

OptBlock0 is the Optimization block 0. Optimizer may choose to divide a query into multiple "parts" and each "part" is optimized individually. OptBlock0 is the block 0 under project.

```
        Generic Tables: ( Gtt0( T1 ) Gti1( T1_I1 ) )
        Generic Columns: ( Gc0(T1 ,Rid) Gc1(T1 ,n2) Gc2(T1
,ind_pad) Gc3(T1 ,n1) Gc4(T1 ,small_vc)) Virtual Generic
Columns: ( )
        Predicates: ( { T1.n1 }  = 2 tc:{3} { T1.ind_pad }
= 'x                                      x' tc:{2} { T1.n2
}  = 3 tc:{1} )
        Transitive Closures: ( Tc0 = { Gc0(T1 ,Rid)} Tc1 =
{ Gc1(T1 ,n2)} Tc2 = { Gc2(T1 ,ind_pad)} Tc3 = { Gc3(T1
,n1)} Tc4 = { Gc4(T1 ,small_vc)} )
```

120

Generic Tables (GT) refer to the underlying table T1 and its index T1_I1 respectively. It is normally a table referenced in a query, but it is also a convenient abstraction to represent any object that is permutated in the join order by the optimizer. For example, a subquery is sometimes modelled as a generic table too. In this case we have one table; Gtt0 T1 and one index; Gti1 T1_I1.

Generic Columns refer to the column level data flow. It is normally just a column of a table referenced in a query, but also an abstraction that includes interesting expressions e.g. those that can be used in an expression join. The first GC is Gc0 (T1, Rid (read RID or Row ID) and the rest are the columns used in the query.

The **Virtual Generic Columns** are generic columns created on interesting expressions and are empty in this example.

The **Predicates** line list the predicates used in the WHERE clause referring to the three columns T1.n1, T1.ind_pad and T1.n2

The line **Transitive Closures** refers to the transitive closures. The optimizer can use a mechanism known as *transitive closure* to generate a few predicates that will only show up in the execution plan. *Transitive closure works by logical inference*. For example, assume that we have two predicates like below

```
        n1 = 159
and     n2 = n1
```

The optimizer will be able to create the predicate

```
    n2 = 159
```

and include that in its calculations. This is called *Transitive Closure*

With Transitive Closure there can be a catch. As the optimizer introduces the predicate with the constant, the optimizer may be allowed to eliminate the predicate without the constant, so that the final *where* clause looks like the following:

```
        n1 = 159
and     n2 = 159
```

> This can be useful in some cases, but it can have some potential side effects.

Reading the next line we have

```
            BEGIN: Search Space Traversal for OptBlock0
```

This means that the optimizer is considering all possible solutions for the Query Execution Plan. These include the Algebraic Space (Trees built with algebraic operator) and Method Structure Space (each node annotated with implementation method).

```
Scan plans selected for this optblock:
```

This line refers to the Query Execution Plans select for *OptBlock0*.

```
Beginning selection of qualifying indexes for table 'T1',
```

This is self explanatory.

```
Estimating selectivity of index 'T1_I1', indid 2
```

This is now getting more familiar to us. The optimizer is considering the access path and looking at the indid 2; T1_I1. Remember that indid = 0 is the table itself and indid = 1 is the clustered index in allpages table.

```
    n1 = 2
    ind_pad = 'x                                              x'
    n2 = 3
    Estimated selectivity for n1,
        selectivity = 0.04001347,
    Estimated selectivity for ind_pad,
        selectivity = 1,
    Estimated selectivity for n2,
        selectivity = 0.0499879,
```

The list of predicates is displayed. Starting with column *n1*, the estimated selectivity is 0.04001347, pretty much what we expect i.e. 0.0.4 (1/25 for 25 distinct values). Not surprisingly the selectivity for column *ind_pad* is 1. Well we only have one distinct value in this column. For *n2* the selectivity is 0.0499879. We estimate this to be 0.05 (1/20 for 20 distinct values).

122

```
     scan selectivity 0.002010552, filter selectivity
0.002010552
     201.0552 rows, 1.031413 pages
```

The optimizer estimates the *scan and filter selectivities* to be
0.002010552. These two parameters predate ASE 15. However, for the
benefit of everyone, we need to understand what *scan* and *filter
selectivities* refer to.

Simply put the **scan selectivity** refers to the *number of index rows and
leaf-level pages to be read.* In contrast, **filter selectivity** is the *number of
data pages to be accessed.* In our example these two parameters are the
same because we have supplied a search argument (SARG) to every
column in the index with no other predicates. This means no more filtering
needs to be done. From these two selectivities, the optimizer estimates to
return 201.0552 rows.

Going back to the scan and index selectivities, if we only supplied
the search arguments for columns *n1* and *n2* and omit column
ind_pad, then these two selectivities would have been different. As
an example

```
Estimating selectivity of index 'T1_I1', indid 2
     n1 = 2
     n2 = 3
     Estimated selectivity for n1,
          selectivity = 0.04001347,
     Estimated selectivity for n2,
          selectivity = 0.0499879,
     scan selectivity 0.04001347, filter
selectivity 0.002010552
```

What you see here is that scan selectivity is basically the selectivity
of the prefix column *n1*. That makes sense since no predicate has
been specified for the index's second column *ind_pad*. This means
that the predicates alone cannot provide the full selectivity and as
such further filtering will be needed.

```
     Data Row Cluster Ratio 0.006930023
     Index Page Cluster Ratio 0.1428571
     Data Page Cluster Ratio 0.00923991
```

From the above output we can see that the optimizer picks up what we got out from the optdiag output for the index itself. Visiting the old ground:

The *Data Row Cluster Ratio* (DRCR) is used to estimate the number of pages that need to be read while using this index to access the data pages. It really applies to the clustered index in an APL or a placement index on a DOL table. For other type of indexes like this one it can be very low.

The *Index Page Cluster Ratio* (IPCR) measures the packing and sequencing of index leaf pages on extents for non-clustered indexes and clustered indexes on DOL tables. For queries that need to read more than one leaf page, the leaf level of the index is scanned using next-page or previous-page pointers. If many leaf rows need to be read, 16K I/O can be used on the leaf pages to read one extent at a time, which makes it very fast. The index page cluster ratio measures fragmentation of the page chain for the leaf level of the index.

The *Data Page Cluster Ratio* (DPCR) is used to estimate the cost of reading a large number of index leaf pages using large I/O. This value is used when costing large I/O for non-clustered indexes and all indexes on a DOL table.

```
    using no index prefetch (size 2K I/O)
    in index cache 'default data cache' (cacheid 0) with LRU
replacement

    using table prefetch (size 16K I/O)
    in data cache 'default data cache' (cacheid 0) with LRU
replacement
```

The optimizer is telling us that the index access will be performed without prefetch, whilst the table access will use prefetch.

 Asynchronous prefetch is part of I/O improvement in ASE. It allows ASE to issue multiple asynchronous physical reads of large buffers from the base table before the query needs them so that most data pages are in cache by the time query processing needs to access the pages. The asynchronous prefetch operation also reduces the times that the task has to wait for the completion of physical read operations. Prefetching improves the performance of sequential scans, such as table scans, clustered and non-clustered index scans, update statistics commands, dbcc checks, some recovery tasks, and queries that access large numbers of pages. Obviously this is valid as long as the I/O subsystem on the host is not saturated.

```
Data Page LIO for 'T1_I1' on table 'T1' = 200.6619
```

This tells us the Data page logical I/O costing for the index.

The next step is for the optimizer to consider the selectivity using the table itself. This is the alternative access path that the optimizer considers.

```
Estimating selectivity for table 'T1'
    Table scan cost is 100000 rows, 14286 pages,
```

Starting with selectivity for the table, it is identified as having 100,000 rows and 14,286 pages

```
The table (Datarows) has 100000 rows, 14286 pages,
Data Page Cluster Ratio 0.9994400
```

Note the Data Page Cluster Ration (DPCR) of 0.9994400 for the table above. This is distinctively different from the DPCR for the index which we saw and it was 0.00923991. For a DOL table like this table, DPCR measures how well the pages are packed on the extents. This high value means complete packing of extents in data pages of this table.

```
n1 = 2
Estimated selectivity for n1,
    selectivity = 0.04001347,
ind_pad = 'x                                                    x'
Estimated selectivity for ind_pad,
    selectivity = 1,
n2 = 3
Estimated selectivity for n2,
    selectivity = 0.0499879,
Search argument selectivity is 0.002010552.
using table prefetch (size 16K I/O)
```

```
    in data cache 'default data cache' (cacheid 0) with LRU
replacement
```

Note that the search argument selectivity is 0.002010552, the same as the filter selectivity that we saw earlier.

```
OptBlock0 Eqc{0} -> Pops added:
```

Earlier on, I mentioned that **OptBlock** is the optimization block. **Eqc** is the *Equivalence class*. It describes the sub-plans that combine a given subset of tables. In this line the optimizer is telling us that all the physical operators for the access path i.e. the index scan and table scan have been considered.

```
        ( PopRidJoin ( PopIndScan T1_I1 T1 ) ) cost:
[C=5106.991 A=5465.069 1] O(L200.6619,P197.6674,C201.0553)
props: [ord:{} Round:1{}]
```

PopRidJoin refers to the Pop joining the index to the table through the *Row ID*. This follows the index scan operator **PopIndScan**. Remember, each operator's output is the input to its parent operator. Here *PopRidJoin* is the parent operator of *PopIndScan* that provides the RID

The **cost** has the estimated costing information for the subplan. **C=** is the *critical path cost of a parallel plan*. **A=** is the *average cost of a parallel plan*. The example here is the format for the parallel costing output.

The **0(L.., P.., C..)** is the logical I/O, Physical I/O and CPU numbers for the top operator under serial costing.

props: [ord:{} Round:1{}] means there is no useful ordering provided by this subplan and the partition property of the top operator is a round robin degree 1 partitioning (basically no partitioning). Note that an ordering could come from either sorting or an Index scan.

An index stores an ordered replica of a subset of the information stored in the rows of a table, as well as a pointer to the source row (Row ID). In this sense **an index is just a collection of *pairs of key and location***. The key is the word by which we are looking. In the case of a book, the location is the page number. In the case of a database, it is the physical row identifier. Looking for a record in a

> table by physical row identifier has **constant complexity,** that is, it does not depend on the number of rows in the table. On the contrary, *Keys in an index are sorted*, so we do not have to read all keys to find the right one. Indeed, searching in an index has ***logarithmic complexity***. If looking for a record in a B-tree index of 1000 records takes 100 ms, it may take 200 ms in an index of million of rows and 300 ms in an index of billion of rows.

Next we have

```
~~~~~~~~~~~~~~~~~~~~~~~~~~~~~~~~~~~~~~~~~~~~~~~~~~~~~~~~~~~~~~~~~~~~~
~~~~~~~~~~~~~~
         BEGIN: APPLYING EXHAUSTIVE SEARCH STRATEGY TO OBTAIN BEST PLAN
~~~~~~~~~~~~~~~~~~~~~~~~~~~~~~~~~~~~~~~~~~~~~~~~~~~~~~~~~~~~~~~~~~~~~

~~~~~~~~~~~~~~~~~~~~~~~~~~~~~~~~~~~~~~~~~~~~~~~~~~~~~~~~~~~~~~~~~~~~~
         DONE: APPLYING EXHAUSTIVE SEARCH STRATEGY TO OBTAIN BEST PLAN
~~~~~~~~~~~~~~~~~~~~~~~~~~~~~~~~~~~~~~~~~~~~~~~~~~~~~~~~~~~~~~~~~~~~~

The best plan found in OptBlock0 :

( PopRidJoin cost: [C=5106.991 A=5465.069 1]
O(L200.6619,P197.6674,C201.0553) props: [ord:{} Round:1{}] (
PopIndScan cost: [C=81.019 A=101.9537 1]
O(L3.031413,P3.031413,C201.0553) props: [ord:{} Round:1{}]
Gti1( T1_I1 ) Gtt0( T1 ) ) cost: [C=81.019 A=101.9537 1]
O(L3.031413,P3.031413,C201.0553) props:  [ord:{} Round:1{}]
) cost: [C=5106.991 A=5465.069 1]
O(L200.6619,P197.6674,C201.0553) props: [ord:{} Round:1{}]

*****************************************************************
***
         DONE: Search Space Traversal for OptBlock0
*****************************************************************
***
```

The optimizer then describes the best plan found in this block. It gives the breakdown of costing for the parent operator **PopRidJoin** and the child operator **PopIndScan**. Note that the lion share of costing comes from retrieving the rows from the base table (i.e. cost associated with *PopRidJoin* = <5465.069> compared to the access path *PopIndScan* = <101.9537>.

```
The Abstract Plan (AP) of the final query execution plan:
```

```
( i_scan T1_I1 T1 ) ( prop T1 ( parallel 1 ) ( prefetch 2 )
( lru ) )
To experiment with the optimizer behavior, this AP can be
modified and then passed to the optimizer using the PLAN
clause: SELECT/INSERT/DELETE/UPDATE
... PLAN '( ... )
```

In this section the optimizer talks about the Abstract Plans (AP). For
example, besides the abstract plans, if you chose to force an index, it will
be shown in here.

```
The best global plan (Pop tree) :

PARALLEL:
        number of worker processes = 12
        max parallel degree = 12
        min(configured,set) parallel degree = 12
        min(configured,set) hash scan parallel degree = 12
        max repartition degree = 1
        resource granularity (percentage) = 10
```

In this section the optimizer summarizes its findings and displays server-
wide parameter settings for parallel queries.

```
FINAL PLAN ( total cost = 5465.069)
        Path: 5106.991
        Work: 5465.069
        Est: 10572.06
```

This is *parallel costing* output.

Path is the *C=* or the *critical path cost of a parallel plan.* *Work* is the
A= which is the *average cost of a parallel plan.* *Est* is the sum of Path
and Work. *It is the estimated cost value used to compare different
plans/subplans*.

Total cost is a serialized version of the parallel cost, mostly only for
diagnostics purpose and I do not think it is of much use to us.

The remaining output is showing the best plan chosen by the optimizer. It
is like the showplan output, but it is a Pop tree with detailed properties for

128

each operator. Some properties are the same as the one you see in the search engine diagnostics output. Please see my comments specified by ← below

```
( PopEmit   ← This is always the top operator

       proj: {{ T1.small_vc } } ← projection of the
operator

       pred: [Tc{} Pe{}] ← predicates of the operator,
there are
                       two kinds of predicates (design
related
                       only)
       subs: {} ← substitution list of the operator,
typically for
                       the base table column on the scan or
virtual
                       expression generic column evaluation.
       cost: [ ← costing information of the operator

              path: 0
              work: 0
              est: 0
       ]
       I/O estimate : [ ← I/O related estimates of the
operator

              rowcount=201.0552 ← estimated row count of
the
                                operator output
              averagewidth=17 ← estimated row width of
the operator
                                output

              pages=1
              lio=0 pio=0 cpu=0
              total lio=0 total pio=0 total cpu=0
       ]
       Cache Strategy: [  ← Fetching data from the table
itself
              prefetch=YES
              iosize=16384 Bytes
```

```
                bufreplace=LRU
        ]
                order: {}
    part: Round Ptn, Degree(s):[ 1 ], TcId's:[ ] ←
partition property

    ( PopRidJoin ← when ASE code generates a Pop plan into
Lava plan, if a PopRidJoin is the immediate parent of the
PopIndScan (as in this case), they are combined into a
single Index Scan lava operator that will fetch data from
both the index and data pages

                proj: {{ T1.small_vc } }
                pred: [Tc{} Pe{{ T1.n1 }  = 2,{ T1.ind_pad }
= 'x                                   x',{ T1.n2 }  =
3}]

                subs: {T1.n2 ,T1.ind_pad ,T1.n1 ,T1.small_vc
}

                cost: [
                        path: 5106.045
                        work: 5464.117
                        est: 10570.16
                ]
                I/O estimate : [
                        rowcount=201.0552
                        averagewidth=17
                        pages=200.6619
                        lio=200.6619 pio=197.6337
cpu=201.0552

                        scanlio=0 scanpio=0 scancpu=0
                ]
                Cache Strategy: [
                        prefetch=YES
                        iosize=16384 Bytes
                        bufreplace=LRU
                ]
                order: {}
                part: Round Ptn, Degree(s):[ 1 ], TcId's:[ ]

                ( PopIndScan index: Gti1( T1_I1 )
                            table: Gtt0( T1 )

                        proj: {{ T1.Rid } ,{ T1.n2 } ,{
T1.ind_pad } ,{ T1.n1 } }
```

130

```
                                        pred:  [Tc{}  Pe{{  T1.n1  }  =  2,{
T1.ind_pad  }  =  'x                                                x',{
T1.n2  }  =  3}]
                                        subs:  {T1.Rid  ,T1.n2  ,T1.ind_pad
,T1.n1  }
                                        cost:  [
                                                path:  80.91687
                                                work:  101.8451
                                                est:  182.762
                                        ]
                                        I/O  estimate  :  [
                                                rowcount=201.0552
                                                averagewidth=17
                                                pages=1.027392
                                                lio=3.027392  pio=3.027392
cpu=201.0552
                                                scanlio=0  scanpio=0
scancpu=0
                                        ]
                                        Cache  Strategy:  [
                                                prefetch=NO
                                                iosize=2048  Bytes
                                                bufreplace=LRU
                                        ]
                                        order:  {}
                                        part:  Round  Ptn,  Degree(s):[  1  ],
TcId's:[  ]
                                  )
              )
  )
```

So far we covered details of the optimizer dealing with the case of simple selectivity. Let us consider a query dealing with *hash joins*. We take a simple example of DEPT and EMP tables. First let us define these two tables:

```
CREATE  TABLE  DEPT  (
   DEPTNO              SMALLINT           NOT  NULL,
   DNAME               VARCHAR  (14)      NULL,
   LOC                 VARCHAR  (13)      NULL
   )
LOCK  datarows
go
ALTER  TABLE  DEPT  ADD  CONSTRAINT  DEPT  PK  PRIMARY  KEY  (DEPTNO)
go
CREATE  TABLE  EMP  (
```

```
   EMPNO            SMALLINT          NOT NULL,
   ENAME            VARCHAR (10)      NULL,
   JOB              VARCHAR (9)       NULL,
   MGR              SMALLINT          NULL,
   HIREDATE         DATE              NULL,
   SAL              NUMERIC(7,2)      NULL,
   COMM             NUMERIC(7,2)      NULL,
   DEPTNO           SMALLINT          NOT NULL
   )
LOCK datarows
go
ALTER TABLE EMP ADD CONSTRAINT EMP PK PRIMARY KEY (EMPNO)
go
ALTER TABLE EMP ADD CONSTRAINT EMP FK
 FOREIGN KEY (DEPTNO)
  REFERENCES DEPT(DEPTNO)
go
```

The construction of these two tables is very simple. A DEPT can have many EMP records. The EMP table has a foreign key constraint EMP_FK. Note that the foreign key constraint does not by default create any index on the child table. DEPT table has 500 rows. In contrast, EMP table has 10,000 rows. Notice that at this instance I am joining a smaller table of 500 rows with another with 10,000 rows. We can write a very simple stored procedure to do the join:

```
create proc sp default
as
begin
select *
  from EMP, DEPT
 where EMP.DEPTNO = DEPT.DEPTNO
end
go
```

As I mentioned we will force the optimizer to use hash-join for this operation. We would like to think that we have a valid case for selecting this join type. Here we have an equijoin operator with the operand *where EMP.DEPTNO = DEPT.DEPTNO*. We are trying to join a small table DEPT with 500 records to the EMP table with 10,000 records and there is no suitable index on the join predicate on the EMP table. Since the existing indexes do not serve this query well, a hash join has its place (to be qualified by the amount of ASE resources available). In a way, this is not surprising, given that the hash table in a hash join is nothing but an in-memory on-demand index with the associated buckets. Contrast this with the worktable that is associated with nested loop join. Unlike an in-

132

memory-table, a worktable is still a physical table, created on the system segment of tempdb. Additionally I should state here that one big benefit of a hash join versus nested loop join (when hash join is useful) comes from the fact that the hash join only needs to read the operands once, while nested loop join has to search the inner operand for EACH outer row. So if you have a very high joinability, nested loop join could be very poorly performing even when you do have all the indexes available!

To force the optimizer to use hash join, we will use the following switches:

```
set nl_join off
set merge_join off
set hash_join on
```

And run the query above and see what happens:

```
         The type of query is SELECT.

ROOT:EMIT Operator

    |HASH JOIN Operator (Join Type: Inner Join)
    |  Using Worktable1 for internal storage.
    |
    |    |SCAN Operator
    |    |  FROM TABLE
    |    |  DEPT
    |    |  Using Clustered Index.
    |    |  Index : DEPT PK
    |    |  Forward Scan.
    |    |  Positioning at index start.
    |    |  Using I/O Size 16 Kbytes for index leaf pages.
    |    |  With LRU Buffer Replacement Strategy for index leaf pages.
    |    |  Using I/O Size 16 Kbytes for data pages.
    |    |  With LRU Buffer Replacement Strategy for data pages.
    |
    |    |SCAN Operator
    |    |  FROM TABLE
    |    |  EMP
    |    |  Table Scan.
    |    |  Forward Scan.
    |    |  Positioning at start of table.
    |    |  Using I/O Size 16 Kbytes for data pages.
    |    |  With LRU Buffer Replacement Strategy for data pages.
```

We now see the Lava Operator Tree output as shown below: The process starts by using DEPT table as the build input with EMP being the probe input.

```
===================== Lava Operator Tree =====================

                    Emit
                  (VA = 3)
```

133

```
                            rows: 9999 est: 9999
                            cpu: 0




                   /
              HashJoin
              Inner Join
              (VA = 2)
              rows: 9999 est: 9999
              lio: 5 est: 5
              pio: 0 est: 0
              bufct: 128
   /                        \
IndexScan                TableScan
DEPT PK                  EMP
(VA = 0)                 (VA = 1)
rows: 500 est: 500       rows: 9999 est: 9999
lio: 12 est: 13          lio: 274 est: 274
pio: 0 est: 7            pio: 0 est: 35

===============================================================
Table: DEPT scan count 1, logical reads: (regular=12 apf=0 total=12),
physical reads: (regular=0 apf=0 total=0), apf IOs used=0
Table: EMP scan count 1, logical reads: (regular=274 apf=0 total=274),
physical reads: (regular=0 apf=0 total=0), apf IOs used=0 Total actual I/O
cost for this command: 572.
Total writes for this command: 0

Execution Time 0.
SQL Server cpu time: 0 ms.  SQL Server elapsed time: 440 ms.

(9999 rows affected)
(return status = 0)
Total actual I/O cost for this command: 0.
Total writes for this command: 0

Execution Time 0.
SQL Server cpu time: 0 ms.  SQL Server elapsed time: 440 ms.

Execution Time 0.
SQL Server cpu time: 0 ms.  SQL Server elapsed time: 476 ms.
```

The number of logical reads has been reduced substantially. It is pretty impressive.

Optimizer Goal	Elasped/CPU/Wait time(ms)	Logical I/O	Physical I/O
Hash-join	476/0/476	291	0

To illustrate the use of hash join further, let me drop all the constraints on both the DEPT and EMP tables and effectively create two bare tables

```
1> alter table EMP drop constraint EMP_FK
2> go
1> alter table EMP drop constraint EMP_PK
```

134

```
2> go
1> alter table DEPT drop constraint DEPT_PK
2> go
```

Let us see what hash join is going to do. As expected the optimizer performs a table scan of the build table EMP. Indeed a table scan costs more and less the same as using the index on this table

```
          The type of query is SELECT.
ROOT:EMIT Operator

    |HASH JOIN Operator (Join Type: Inner Join)
    | Using Worktable1 for internal storage.
    |
    |    |SCAN Operator
    |    | FROM TABLE
    |    | DEPT
    |    | Table Scan.
    |    | Forward Scan.
    |    | Positioning at start of table.
    |    | Using I/O Size 16 Kbytes for data pages.
    |    | With LRU Buffer Replacement Strategy for data pages.
    |
    |    |SCAN Operator
    |    | FROM TABLE
    |    | EMP
    |    | Table Scan.
    |    | Forward Scan.
    |    | Positioning at start of table.
    |    | Using I/O Size 16 Kbytes for data pages.
    |    | With LRU Buffer Replacement Strategy for data pages.
```

With the Lava Operator Tree

```
==================== Lava Operator Tree ====================

                         Emit
                         (VA = 3)
                         rows: 9999 est: 9999
                         cpu: 0


              /
            HashJoin
            Inner Join
            (VA = 2)
            rows: 9999 est: 9999
            lio: 5 est: 5
            pio: 0 est: 0
            bufct: 128
   /                        \
TableScan                 TableScan
DEPT                      EMP
(VA = 0)                  (VA = 1)
```

```
rows: 500 est: 500       rows: 9999 est: 9999
lio: 11 est: 11          lio: 274 est: 274
pio: 0 est: 2            pio: 0 est: 35


==============================================================
Table: DEPT scan count 1, logical reads: (regular=11 apf=0 total=11),
physical reads: (regular=0 apf=0 total=0), apf IOs used=0
Table: EMP scan count 1, logical reads: (regular=274 apf=0 total=274),
physical reads: (regular=0 apf=0 total=0), apf IOs used=0 Total actual I/O
cost for this command: 570.
Total writes for this command: 0

Execution Time 0.
SQL Server cpu time: 0 ms.  SQL Server elapsed time: 420 ms.

(9999 rows affected)
(return status = 0)
Total actual I/O cost for this command: 0.
Total writes for this command: 0

Execution Time 0.
SQL Server cpu time: 0 ms.  SQL Server elapsed time: 420 ms.

Execution Time 0.
SQL Server cpu time: 0 ms.  SQL Server elapsed time: 456 ms.
```

With the summary results

Optimizer Goal	Elasped/CPU/Wait time (ms)	Logical I/O	Physical I/O
Hash-join no index	456/0/456	290	0

How does this work? First the optimizer takes the DEPT table as the build input. The table scan on 500 rows involves 11 lio. DEPT.DEPTNO is unique. If we have the mod(DEPT.DEPTNO,20) we are going to get 20 offset values each with 25 entries. You can easily verify this one by working out DEPT.DEPTNO%20 in sql for DEPTNO values between 1 and 500. So effectively what we are getting here is 25 linked lists for every offset in the hash table.

After this, the second phase *probing* is performed. In the probing phase, the table EMP is read sequentially and for each record in this table the matching records in the DEPT are retrieved from the build input buckets. The projection is then sent back to the Emit operator. Note that probing can be done at a constant cost because DEPT input is now in memory and has a hash access path on the join attributes. We see that scanning the EMP table involves 274 lio and the hash join operator only needs 5 lio to complete this work.

Summary of dealing with ASE 15 optimizer

I hope that the above examples covered some aspects of ASE 15 optimizer and how to interpret showplan and Lava operator tree. Key points to remember are as follows:

- Understanding the concept of Logical and Physical Operators and of the Lava Query Engine
- Understanding the detailed showplan output, especially the terminologies and Operators that the Lava Query Engine uses
- The typical cost of using a B-tree index, the scan selectivity and the filter selectivity
- Coverage of hash joins in ASE 15
- The importance of keeping *statistics* run up-to-date
- Practical application of optimizer

The most common problems observed with ASE 15 optimizer

As per any optimizer there are occasions that optimizer will make a wrong decisions. ASE 15 is no exception. The followings are some examples:

1. If showplan shows an index scan without *Positioning by key*, you need to check whether there is indeed no usable search argument (sarg) ("<col> relop <constant>") on the index prefix column(s) from your query. If you think you do have such sarg, then the index scan could perform much better if the final plan is using the sarg to position the index scan.
2. If showplan shows a UNION/VECTOR AGGREGATE/SORTING subplan within a subquery and the subplan is NOT correlated to the parent query block, it might perform badly if the subquery has to be evaluated many times for different parent query block correlation values. A better plan could choose to materialize those subplan only once into a worktable first outside of the subquery and only reference the worktable in the subquery. For example you can deploy a #table to store the result of subquery and use that #table in the join. This pattern really depends on the actual data distribution. If the subquery rarely needs to be evaluated, the materialization cost may not pay off.

3. If showplan shows SORT operator over large intermediate result and there is no ORDER BY in the query or no obvious parent operator (such as MERGE JOIN) needing the ordering provided by the SORT, the plan could be better without the SORT. This pattern would also depend on the actual data distribution. Bear in mind that SORT could serve other purposes than simply providing the needed ordering.

4. Another potential issue that you may see is ASE stack trace when you are executing a piece of code or stored procedure. You will typically get the usual stack trace in ASE's log

```
00:00000:00161:2009/06/18 09:32:31.72 kernel  Current
process (0x12be0228) infected with signal 11 (SIGSEGV)
00:00000:00161:2009/06/18 09:32:31.72 kernel  Address
0x00000000804c5864 (des_rekeep+0x4), siginfo (code, address)
= (1, 0x0000000000
00029c)
00:00000:00161:2009/06/18 09:32:31.72 kernel
************************************
00:00000:00161:2009/06/18 09:32:31.72 kernel  SQL causing
error : P_GetContract @asset_cd = 'DE0003137790_I'
00:00000:00161:2009/06/18 09:32:31.72 kernel
************************************
```

This may be followed with 6103 error message:

```
00:00000:00161:2009/06/18 09:32:31.74 server  Error: 6103,
Severity: 17, State: 1
00:00000:00161:2009/06/18 09:32:31.74 server  Unable to do
cleanup for the killed process;
```

In most probability you will not be able to drop and recreate the procedure. The only option you will have is to reboot ASE.

ASE 15 Semantic partitioning and data archiving

I mentioned that ASE 15 has an optimiser that is specifically designed for mixed load and addresses the handling of mixed load databases. In addition, ASE 15 offers an additional optional feature called *Semantic or Smart Partitioning*. Partitioning allows a table or index to be subdivided into smaller pieces, where each piece of such a database object is called a partition. Each partition has its own name, and may optionally have its own storage characteristics. The advantages are that these smaller pieces can be managed either collectively or individually. This gives the DBA considerable flexibility in managing partitioned objects. However, from the perspective of the application, a partitioned table is identical to a non-partitioned table; no modifications are necessary when accessing a partitioned table using SQL queries and DML statements. In general you should consider partitioning:

- When the table is greater than 2 GB
- For tables containing historical data, in which new data is added into the newest partition. A typical example is a historical table where only the current month's data is updatable and the other 11 months are read only.
- When the contents of a table need to be distributed across different types of storage devices.

Once partitioned, indexes on the partitioned table can be built locally or globally. This will help

- Avoid rebuilding the entire index when data is removed.
- Perform maintenance on parts (example, updating partition statistics) of the data without invalidating the entire index.
- Reduce the impact of index skew caused by an index on a column with a monotonically increasing value.

Overall, partitioning

- Enables ODSS throughput improvements
- Allows smaller maintenance window due to partition-oriented maintenance
- Adds more to Sybase server availability by virtue of smaller maintenance window
- Can largely eliminate the need for archiving and thus *reduce the development and maintenance cost*. This is an important factor. I will cover it below.

Archiving in a nutshell

I do not intend to cover the technical characteristics of semantic partitioning. Reference [15] covers many technical aspects of this feature. However, most of us have or look after databases that go through some form of archiving, mainly for performance and sizing considerations. For many reasons including the statutory trading and accounting needs, historical data has to be accessible going back few years. For example, in the UK this period is the previous six years plus the current year. Archiving typically subdivides large or very large tables (large being a relative term) in a database into sub tables based on a range criterion like a particular date. The objective is to keep the most recent data in the *current* tables and archive old data to *archive or historical* tables or database.

This will keep the size of the most accessed tables manageable and will improve performance of queries based on the assumption that 80% of the time queries access 20% of data. That twenty percent is normally the most recent data. However, over a period of time archiving will make archive tables much larger and a new archiving strategy has to be devised. Archiving can be done in the current database or another database. More often a parallel strategy has to be devised to enable users to access archived data as well. In some cases additional development work is needed to present both the current and historical data in a seamless manner. This is an expensive process, thus requiring a fair bit of design and development work. In practice some of this effort can b e avoided with partitioning.

Archiving needs to be scheduled periodically, typically once a day or once a week at least, involving certain risk. It will shift a non insignificant amount of data from the current tables to archive tables. A single table may require up to a million records to be deleted from it *daily* and added to its archived counterpart. This archive process has to be written carefully and needs to take the application logic into account. Archiving involves careful analysis work and will require thorough testing. All these are time consuming processes.

A failure in the archiving process (such as when records were removed from the current tables but not added to the archive tables, due to transaction problems), can result in orphaned records, requiring costly

140

recovery procedures involving the offside backups etc. The situation could be compounded by the fact that the missing records may not be detected for a good while, thus adding to the complexity. Additionally, archiving process creates a fair amount of network traffic when replication is used. This adds further loads on the network traffic between the primary and DR and will create some latency between the primary and replicate databases as well.

Potential benefits of partitioning

1. Performance gains including qualitative business benefits perceived by users due to impact of partitioning on large tables
2. Reduced maintenance time
3. Reduced support due to possible elimination of a need for a separate archive database
4. Reduced loss of data due to archiving errors
5. Reduced development time

Partitioning as a substitute for archiving, a case illustration

Let us look at a case of having an application that is centered on a holding table plus a number of auxiliary tables dealing with instruments. I call this table t_holding_analytic and they all belong to an analytic database. In its simplest form archiving moves analytics data i.e. records in t_holding_analytic and others to their archived counterpart. We label these tables t_holding_analytic_hist and so forth. In this example, a while back, upon the review of the application performance, it was decided to archive records older than the current month in the so called historical tables. The analytics generated just over ¼ Million records daily. There were around 5 Million records in t_holding_analytic and around 130 Million records in the archived counterpart table t_holding_analytic_hist. Records in t_holding_analytic corresponded to one month data. So in effect we kept one month's data current and put the rest into historical tables. With ASE partitioning we decided that we may get away with archiving and would not need code specific changes to cater for archive tables. Rather than putting all data more than *a month old* in archived tables, we decided to *range partition* the current tables t_holding_analytic and others, based on effective date *eff_dt* (i.e. the business date that the holding was generated)).

The strategy was to cover one partition for data before 2007 that was seldom needed and then one partition per calendar Month for *eff_dt*. This ensured that data was spread uniformly across all 12 partitions (assuming Jan – Dec 2008) plus one for *eff_dt* < 2008. We used this method as it allowed us to add new partitions as needed. By doing so we removed the need for historical tables and as such some complexities like using dynamic SQL in the procedure code, specific for archiving, could then be avoided. Given the licensing cost of partitioning, we opted for trial license (which we managed to extend few times) and justified the purchasing of the partition option as a future proof investment strategy. To do so we compared the implementation cost for archiving vs. gains from partitioning. Roughly these were translated as follows:

◆ Implementation costs for Archiving

- Developer cost on going
- DBA cost (one off)
- Ongoing additional maintenance cost
- Data recovery cost from failed archiving and subsequent recovery involving offsite backups, DBA time, developer time and possible rerun of batches out of hours

◆ Implementation costs for partitioning

- Licensing cost
- Install license
- Partitioning tables, creating global and local indexes, stats update, verification and testing

◆ Summary Benefits from deploying partitioning

- Reduced development cycle to include archiving
- Improved performance and query response time
- More efficient DBA support
- Reduced maintenance times

142

You can refer to ASE documentation for partition type and syntax. However, in here I will give you an example of range partitioning for table t_holding_analytic_hist.

```
1> alter table t_holding_analytic
2> partition by range (eff_dt)
3> ( p0 values <= ('12/31/07'),
4> p1 values <= ('01/31/08'),
5> p2 values <= ('02/29/08'),
6> p3 values <= ('03/31/08'),
7> p4 values <= ('04/30/08'),
8> p5 values <= ('05/31/08'),
9> p6 values <= ('06/30/08'),
10> p7 values <= ('07/31/08'),
11> p8 values <= ('08/31/08'),
12> p9 values <= ('09/30/08'),
13> p10 values <= ('10/31/08'),
14> p11 values <= ('11/30/08'),
15> p12 values <= ('12/31/08') )
16> go
```

In a similar fashion other tables were partitioned on this *eff_dt* column as well. The next step was to choose a correct indexing strategy with partitioned tables.

Partitioning and indexing strategy

There seems to be some confusion about global and local indexes in partitioned tables. Taking current partitioning scheme, ASE 15 offers the following directives (excluding the traditional round robin partitioning):

1. Range Partitioning Based on consecutive ranges of values. Example Orders table range partitioned by order_date
2. List Partitioning Based on unordered lists of values. Orders table list partitioned by country
3. Hash Partitioning Based on a hash algorithm. Orders table hash partitioned by customer_id

A directive is a physical storage order on the partition. By the same token a *global* clustered index does not make sense on a partitioned table. A clustered index requests physical order of data based on the index values.

143

The table is already physically ordered by the partition key/keys. You cannot have two directives for physically ordering records in a table.

You can create a global unique index which is essentially identical to an index on a nonpartitioned table. The main reason to have this global unique index is to enforce primary key constraints.

All index types are supported on local indexes except for one caveat (see below). A local index has got to be consistent across all partitions. So you cannot have an index on one partition only.

A unique clustered index can only be created as a local index with or without "local index" clause. This unique local clustered index has got to have column or columns (for hash key) on which the partitioning is based on. For example, if the table is range partitioned, the local unique clustered index has got to have the range column as part of its index key. The positioning of the key does not matter in the index hierarchy. However, future enhancements may override this by allowing creating a local unique index where this index's uniqueness is meant for individual partition only and it will not require the partition column(s) to be part of the index keys.

As a side note, when we were doing tests with range partitioning we noticed that if you have a normal non clustered index with index covering, this type of index can outdo and outperform partitioning. We believe this is because when you have an index on the same partition column for an un-partitioned table, any range lookup using the index is like a partitioned search. Of course partitioning though has far more other benefits than this single scenario.

Sybase as yet does not support Composite partitioning such as Range-Range, Range-Hash etc. For example, Orders table range partitioned by order_date and sub-partitioned by hash on customer_id.

A unique clustered index can only be created as a local index with or without "local index" clause. This unique local clustered index has got to have column or columns (for hash key) on which the partitioning is based on. For example, if the table is range partitioned, the local unique clustered index has got to have the range column as part of its index key. The positioning of the key does not matter in the index hierarchy. However, future enhancements may override this by allowing creating a

144

local unique index where this index's uniqueness is meant for individual partition only and it will not require the partition column(s) to be part of the index keys.

Sybase as yet does not support Composite partitioning such as Range-Range, Range-Hash etc. For example, Orders table range partitioned by order_date and sub-partitioned by hash on customer_id.

Conclusion

It is impossible to cover all aspects of the ASE 15 upgrade in a booklet of this size. I am hopeful that there is enough coverage here to allow you to get on with your ASE 15 upgrade process. Remember that good planning is essential for an upgrade task and you will need to consider and plan for all aspects of work.

References

[1] A Winning Strategy: Running the most Critical Financial Data on ASE 15

Mich Talebzadeh, Sybase white paper 2008
http://www.sybase.com/files/Product_Overviews/ASE-Winning-Strategy-091908.pdf

[2] ASE 15.0.x Migration Checklist, Version 1.11

http://www.sybase.com/files/Technical_Documents/Sybase_Migration_Checklistfor_ASE15.x_-_GA_Version_1.1.pdf

[3] Intelligent Statistics Management in Sybase ASE 15.0,

Xiao Ming Zhou et al, ISBN 978-3-540-33337-1.

[4] A closer look at query processing in ASE 15.0

Stefan Karlsson, International Sybase User Group (ISUG) Technical Journal, second quarter 2005

[5] Peter Dorfman, private communication

[6] International Sybase User Group, Sybase-product-future forum

Stefan Karlsson, in reply to the thread by Mich Talebzadeh titled *Role reversal in hash join in ASE 15*, 24th April 2007

[7] Sybase ASE 15 Best Practices: Query Processing & Optimization

Sybase White Paper, Version 1.1 – February 2008

[8] ASE 15.0.2, Performance and Tuning Series: Query Processing and Abstract Plans

Available from the following website:

http://infocenter.sybase.com/help/topic/com.sybase.infocenter.dc00743.1502/pdf/queryprocessing.pdf

[9] ASE 15 special interest discussion Forum. Jeff Tallman, Bill Grant, March 2009

[10] ASE 15.0 Query Performance & Migration Tips & Tricks. Presentation by Jeff Tallman, July 2009. Copies available from jeff.tallman@sybase.com

[11] Ed Barlow, Extended Stored Procedures Library, **http://www.edbarlow.com/gem/procs_only/index.htm**

[12] Jeff Tallman, private communication

[13] Ethernet Maximum Transmission Unit (MTU). See the following link: **http://en.wikipedia.org/wiki/Maximum_transmission_unit**

[14] Fiber Distributed Data Interface (FDDI). See the following link **http://www.pulsewan.com/data101/fddi_basics.htm**

[15] Reducing Maintenance Time & Improving Availability Using Semantic Partitions in ASE 15.0. Sybase technical white paper by Jeff Tallman. Available from the following site: http://www.sybase.com/files/White_Papers/Reducing-Maintenance-ASE-Partitions-042809-WP.pdf

[16] New Features Bulletin Adaptive Server® Enterprise 15.0.2 ESD #4 http://infocenter.sybase.com/help/topic/com.sybase.infocenter.dc00803.1502/pdf/NF1502ESD4.pdf

Index

#

#table, 28, 29, 90, 91, 92, 94, 95, 137

@

@@SPID, 29

3

32-bit, 6, 17, 32, 34, 66

A

Adaptive Server Enterprise, i, 3
append_union_all, 63
archiving, 140, 142
ASE 12.5.2, 25, 38
ASE 12.5.4, 7, 15, 18, 37, 38, 67, 68
ASE 15, i, vii, 3, 4, 5, 6, 7, 8, 9, 10, 11, 14, 15, 16, 17, 18, 19, 20, 21, 22, 23, 25, 27, 28, 29, 31, 32, 33, 34, 36, 37, 38, 40, 52, 53, 54, 65, 66, 67, 68, 69, 73, 75, 76, 77, 79, 81, 88, 97, 98, 103, 104, 105, 106, 112, 123, 137, 138, 143, 145, 146, 147
asynchronous prefetch, 124
Auxiliary Utilities, 65

B

baselining data, 75
benefits, 10, 12, 13, 14, 142
big devices, 31, 98
bigint, 68
bushy_search_space, 64

C

cache utilization, 78
cardinality, 4, 39, 52
catalog contention, 8, 32

Cluster Edition, i, 11
compiled objects, 34, 36, 75
computed columns, 68
Computed Columns, 9
configuration parameters, 5, 23
cost, 5, 8, 11, 12, 14, 22, 52, 55, 59, 71, 105, 112, 115, 116, 117, 118, 119, 120, 124, 125, 126, 127, 128, 129, 130, 131, 134, 136, 137, 139, 142
CPU Time, 80, 86

D

Data Page Cluster Ratio
  DPCR, 116, 123, 124, 125
Data Row Cluster Ratio
  DRCR, 116, 123, 124
Datachange function, 40
datachange(), 6, 40
DBCC CHECKALLOC, 20, 22
dbcc dbrepair, 33
DBCC DBREPAIR, 20, 22
dbcc prsqlcache, 26
dbcc purgesqlcache, 26, 114, 120
dbcc traceon (7730), 29
dbcc upgrade_object, 34, 35
DDL, 8, 68
Decision Support System
  DSS, 3
default network packet size, 23
deferred compilation, 29
Deferred Compilation, 28
deleting statistics, 38, 52
device hit statistics, 98
Disk IO, 31
disk IO structure, 31
distinct_sorted, 64
distinct_sorting, 64

E

Ed Barlow, vii, 82, 98, 147
Elapsed Time, 79, 87

148

Lightning Source UK Ltd.
Milton Keynes UK
30 October 2009

145573UK00001B/38/P